THE NEW STUDENTS' COOKBOOK

By Carolyn Humphries

foulsham
LONDON • NEW YORK • TORONTO • SYDNEY

foulsham

The Publishing House, Bennetts Close,
Cippenham, Slough, Berkshire SL1 5AP, England

ISBN 0-572-02399-5

Copyright © 1997 W. Foulsham & Co. Ltd

Illustrations by Sophie Azimont
Typeset by Grafica, Bournemouth
Printed in Great Britain by Cox & Wyman Ltd, Reading

CONTENTS

FEED ME

INTRODUCTION

When you leave home for the first time and have to fend for yourself, you could be in for a bit of a shock. No Mum to shop, clean or cook for you any more. But surviving on your own or in your shared accommodation isn't really that hard – not with a little help!

This book is designed for anyone who hasn't had to cook for themselves before. It won't insult you by telling you how to open a can of baked beans and put them on toast (mind you, that's a great standby), but it does have masses of tasty, nourishing meals that don't cost a fortune, are dead simple and don't take ages to prepare. It has loads of advice on what to eat to keep fit and well and how to cook the basics such as vegetables, pasta, rice and eggs. It has simple ways to make meals go further if you have friends round, food to eat to keep you going during exams and tasty snacks that can easily turn into main meals to eke out the last of your cash. There's also a simple guide to what you'll need to buy and basic food hygiene. But it won't tell you to keep your room tidy or remind you to do your washing – that's your problem!

Eat well – eat wisely

To enjoy college life to the full (and to help the brain cells work) it is important to eat a healthy diet. That doesn't mean cranky food, just good, balanced meals made up of the following constituents:

- At least five portions of fruit and vegetables a day – any kind, any amount. You need them for vitamins, minerals and general well-being. Many are also cheap, which helps a lot. Eat them cooked or raw, canned, frozen or fresh.

TIP: Market stalls are likely to be cheaper than the supermarket for fresh produce. If you are buying in a supermarket look for economy ranges or buy loose rather than pre-packed – it's cheaper.

- Loads of starchy foods (carbohydrates) for energy and to fill you up. These are bread, potatoes, rice, pasta and breakfast cereals (whole grain varieties such as muesli, porridge, Weetabix or Shredded Wheat rather than sugary ones such as Frosties or Cocopops). They're not fattening in themselves. It's the fats or sugary stuff you put on them that piles on weight.

TIP: Buy supermarket own brands. They're much cheaper.

- At least two portions of protein a day for body growth and repair. These are meat, poultry, fish, eggs, dairy products such as cheese, milk and yoghurt, pulses (dried peas, beans and lentils, including baked beans in tomato sauce) and vegetable protein such as tofu, TVP and Quorn.

TIP: Cheap cuts of meat are just as good for you as expensive ones and all species of fish are nutritious, regardless of cost. But if you go for economy ranges of, say, sausages, they are likely to contain far more rusk filler and be a lot fattier with less actual meat than a good quality one. Read the labels to be sure what you are buying. You will probably enjoy them more and feel just as full after two good sausages as four economy ones!

- A very little fat – essential for body warmth and energy, BUT you don't need masses of extra butter or margarine or gallons of oil for frying. You get most of what you need naturally in other foods, such as dairy products, meat and cereals, so have only a scraping or butter or marge on bread, use the minimum oil for cooking (drain well before eating) and try to grill rather than fry foods where possible.

Equipment essentials

Most furnished accommodation supplies basic kitchen equipment. All being well this will include a cooker with an oven and a fridge with either a freezer or freezing compartment and basic crockery and cutlery. But it's worth making sure you have as many as possible of the following items:

- ★ Chopping board
- ★ Colander for straining cooked vegetables etc
- ★ Flameproof casserole (Dutch oven) with lid – a fairly small one which can be used on top of the stove or in the oven is useful
- ★ Bowls, at least one large for mixing and one pudding basin
- ★ Draining spoon, long-handled and with holes in it
- ★ Fish slice
- ★ Frying pan (skillet)
- ★ Grater
- ★ Kettle
- ★ Kitchen scissors
- ★ Oven gloves
- ★ Ovenproof dish, medium sized
- ★ Paperware – kitchen paper, foil and/or clingfilm (plastic wrap) and, ideally, greaseproof (waxed) paper
- ★ Pastry brush
- ★ Potato masher
- ★ Potato peeler
- ★ Rolling pin (not vital, as a clean bottle will do instead)
- ★ Roasting tins (baking pans), preferably one large and one small
- ★ Sharp knives, at least one small for vegetables etc. and one large for cutting up meat. A bread knife with a serrated edge is also useful

★ Saucepans, ideally one small, one medium and one large, with lids
★ Whisk. A balloon one is ideal for making sauces etc
★ Wooden spoon
★ Scales and measuring spoons/cups
★ Washing up cloths. Packets of disposable ones are best although they can be shoved in the washing machine if times are hard!
★ Pan scourer. The green square ones are best, but avoid those with sponge backs as you can never get rid of all the soap suds! Don't forget washing-up liquid, surface and oven cleaners, too
★ Tea towels (dish cloths) and hand towels

The first big shopping list

Buy all the basics you need at the beginning, then you'll just have to replace odds and ends each week as they run out.

Essential storecupboard items

★ Plain (all-purpose) flour
★ Baking powder
★ Salt
★ Pepper
★ Sugar. Caster (superfine) is OK for most uses, but light brown is useful too
★ Dried mixed herbs. These are essential, ideally plus dried basil, chives, mint, and sage
★ Dried onion flakes and dried red and green (bell) peppers, not vital but great for brightening up rice or pasta and they keep for ages
★ Chilli powder
★ Cayenne
★ Ground cinnamon and/or nutmeg
★ Ground ginger, not essential but useful, especially for Chinese-style dishes
★ Caraway and poppy seeds, not essential but useful for adding a quite distinctive flavour

★ Tube of tomato purée (paste)
★ Tube of garlic purée (paste) – much easier than fiddling around crushing cloves
★ Curry powder and curry paste
★ Vinegar, any sort – I use white or red wine vinegar, but white distilled or malt are OK
★ Lemon juice – not vital but a bottle will keep in the fridge for ages and is often better than vinegar in many recipes
★ Stock cubes – vegetable and/or chicken
★ Table sauces – ketchup (catsup), brown, Worcestershire and soy sauces
★ Mustard – English and Dijon are the most useful
★ Oil – sunflower or good quality vegetable oil
★ Marmalade
★ Marmite (Vegemite) or other yeast extract – good as a drink made with boiling water, as well as on toast and for flavour instead of stock cubes. Also highly nutritious!
★ Mayonnaise or salad cream
★ Honey
★ Long-grain rice
★ Pasta – quick-cook macaroni or other shapes, spaghetti, lasagne sheets, stuffed dried tortellini
★ Packet processed cheese – useful but not essential
★ Packet sponge cake mix – useful but not essential
★ Packet stuffing mix – useful but not essential
★ Breakfast cereal – choose a whole grain one such as Weetabix, Shredded Wheat or muesli rather than a sweet, sugary one. It'll fill you up for longer
★ Dried milk (non-fat dry milk) is useful for cooking (but not so good for drinking, except in coffee or tea)
★ Raisins and sultanas (golden raisins) – good for snacking, on cereals and in lots of recipes
★ Instant mashed potato powder – useful for thickening

TIP: Keep any dregs of wine or beer for cooking – it does wonders for the flavour of many a soup or stew.

Canny cans

★ Tomatoes – some brands of whole plum tomatoes are incredibly cheap, while well-known brands and ready chopped ones are much more expensive
★ Baked beans
★ Pulses – red kidney beans, butter beans, cannellini beans etc.
★ Sweetcorn (corn)
★ Peas, carrots, green beans – useful to keep for some of the recipes and for quick accompaniments
★ Tuna – supermarkets have very low-price cans, if you avoid the top brands. Check the label for the 'dolphin-friendly' symbol.
★ Mackerel, pilchards or sardines
★ Condensed mushroom, chicken and tomato soup – ideal for sauces
★ Minced and/or stewed steak
★ Hot dogs (frankfurters)
★ Any canned fruit – pineapple is very useful in cooking
★ Rice pudding
★ Custard

Perishables

★ Reduced fat spread – check the label to make sure it is suitable for spreading and cooking (I've called it margarine in the recipes)
★ Medium eggs
★ Bread/rolls/pitta bread/naan bread – store in the freezer and take out as required. Sliced bread can be toasted straight from frozen if you forget to take it out in time
★ Cheese – choose a strong-flavoured one for cooking, then you don't need to use so much to get the right taste
★ Plain yoghurt – good for sauces and dressings as well as for breakfast with cereal or with honey or fruit for dessert
★ Milk – keep a carton in the freezer so you won't run out; it does take ages to thaw though, and will need a good shake once defrosted. Alternatively, keep a carton of long-life milk in your cupboard
★ Frozen peas/beans

Everyday fruit and veg
- ★ Apples
- ★ Oranges/satsumas/clementines
- ★ Bananas
- ★ Potatoes
- ★ Carrots
- ★ Onions
- ★ Salad stuff (keep in the fridge)
- ★ Cabbage (especially white or savoy) is good shredded for salad as well as cooked

Basic preparation

Whenever you read a cookery book, it tells you to prepare various ingredients but it doesn't tell you how – until now.

Beat: Hold the bowl or pan in your left hand (or right if you're left-handed) and tilt slightly. Hold a wooden spoon in your other hand and stir the contents round fast and firmly in one direction until smooth.

Chop: It's usually best to cut any vegetable or fruit in half first so the flat cut side is down on the chopping board. Then hold firmly in one hand and, using a sharp knife, make cuts at even distances along the length of the food not quite through one end. Then, still holding it together, make cuts across it so that it is cut into small pieces. To chop finely, simply make the cuts closer together. To chop coarsely, make them wider apart.

TIP: To chop fresh herbs, put them in a cup and snip with scissors for best results.

Dice: Much like chopping but into bigger cubes and you can cut right through the food at both ends as it's easier to hold together.

Fold: Usually used when mixing a light, airy mixture. Use a metal spoon and gently cut and turn over the mixture using a figure-of-eight motion.

Grate: Hold the grater firmly in one hand over a plate and rub the ingredient to be grated up and down the appropriate side of the grater. To grate coarsely (as for cheese, carrots or chocolate for instance) use the side with the largest holes. To grate finely (as for lemon and other citrus rind) use the middle-sized holes, and for grating to a powder (for whole nutmeg) use the finest holes.

Knead: (Usually of dough.) Gently work the mixture together to a ball with your hands, then turn on to a board and squeeze and press the mixture until it forms a ball without any cracks.

Mash: Use a potato masher or fork. Press the ingredient against the sides of the bowl or saucepan so it is forced through the gaps in the fork or masher to form a smoothish paste.

TIP: For potatoes give them a good beat with the masher once mashed to make them fluffy.

Pare: Cut thin shreds of rind off something with a small, sharp knife (serrated is often best).

Roll: (Usually of pastry or other dough.) Place the dough on a board, dusted with flour, and roll firmly but evenly with a rolling pin (or clean milk or wine bottle), always rolling away from you. Give the dough a quarter turn and repeat. Never roll from side to side as it stretches the dough which will then shrink on cooking.

Separate an egg: The easiest way is to break the egg on to a saucer. Then hold an egg cup over the yolk and strain the white into a separate container.

Whip/whisk: Use a balloon whisk to beat the mixture in a circular motion, making sure you lift the mixture up with the whisk as you go to incorporate as much air as possible.

Basic cooking skills

The old chestnut 'He can't even boil an egg' isn't so funny – many people can't! Here are some simple instructions for all the basic foods you'll want to cook.

Eggs

Boiled: An egg pricker which you can buy in hardware shops is a great little gadget. You pierce the air sac end of the egg and it prevents it cracking when boiling. Place the egg(s) in a small saucepan and just cover with cold water. Cover with a lid (for quicker boiling) and bring to the boil. As soon as the water boils, start your timer and cook for 3–4 minutes for runny yolks and firm whites, 5–6 minutes for hard-boiled (hard-cooked).

TIP: For hard-boiled eggs to eat cold, plunge them immediately into cold water after cooking to prevent a black ring forming round the yolks.

Fried: Heat a very little oil in a frying pan (skillet). Break each egg into a cup and gently slide into the hot oil. Spoon a little oil over the eggs as they fry and remove with a fish slice as soon as cooked to your liking.

Poached: Bring a frying pan (skillet) of water to simmering point and add 15 ml/1 tbsp of vinegar or lemon juice. Break each egg into a cup and then gently slide into the simmering water. Cook for 3 minutes for soft yolks, 4–5 minutes for hard. Do not allow to boil rapidly or the white will break up. Lift out with a fish slice.

Scrambled: Heat a knob of margarine and 15 ml/1 tbsp of milk for each egg in a saucepan. Whisk in the eggs with a balloon whisk or fork. When well blended, add a little salt and pepper and cook over a gentle heat, stirring all the time until the mixture scrambles but is still creamy. Do not allow to boil or the mixture will go rubbery and watery. Serve immediately and soak the pan in hot soapy water straight away or it will be horrible to clean!

Omelette: See individual recipes (pages 32, 55, 56).

Potatoes

Boiled: Peel or scrub and cut into even-sized pieces. Place in a pan with just enough cold water to cover. Add salt, if liked. Part-cover with a lid, bring to the boil, reduce the heat slightly and boil quickly until tender (about 10 minutes, depending on the size of the pieces). Drain and use as required.

Chipped: Peel, if liked, and cut each potato into finger-thick slices. Then cut each slice into chips. Pat dry on kitchen paper or on a clean tea towel (dish cloth). Heat enough oil to three-quarters fill the frying pan (skillet), or at least 2.5 cm/1 in in a saucepan (or use a chip pan if you have one). To test the temperature, slide in one chip down the back of the fish slice into the oil. If it starts to sizzle immediately, the oil is ready. Gently slide the chips down the fish slice into the pan a handful at a time, and spread then out with the slice. Cook until golden and soft in the centre. Don't add more chips than the pan will hold comfortably. If they are packed in and sticking out of the oil the temperature will drop too much and they will stew rather than fry crisply. Better to cook two batches if necessary. Drain on kitchen paper before serving.

Crispy potato skins: Scrub the potatoes, then peel fairly thickly. (Submerge the peeled potatoes in cold water to cook for the next meal.) Sprinkle a thin layer of salt on a baking sheet and lay the peelings on top. Bake in a preheated oven at 200°C/440°F/gas mark 6 for about 20 minutes until crispy. Toss and serve hot or cold.

Alternatively, cut the potatoes in halves lengthways and boil for about 10–15 minutes or until soft. Scoop out the potato into a bowl (where it can be mashed and saved for your next meal), leaving a thick 'shell' about 1 cm/½ in thick. Cut each shell into three or four wedges, then deep fry as for chips (see above) for 2–3 minutes until crisp and golden. Drain on kitchen paper, then season with salt and a dash of chilli powder, if liked. Serve hot.

Jacket-baked: Scrub, leave whole and prick all over with a fork. Rub with oil and salt (if liked) and place directly in the middle shelf of the oven. Bake at 180°C/350°F/gas mark 4 for about 1 hour or until the potatoes feel soft when squeezed with an oven-gloved hand. The oven temperature isn't vital; cook for longer in a slower oven or for less time in a hotter oven.

TIP: If you thread the potatoes on to metal skewers they will cook more quickly as the heat is conducted through the centres.

Mashed: Prepare as for boiled but always peel first. Once boiled, strain off the water, then add a knob of margarine and a dash of milk. Mash with a potato masher or fork until smooth, then beat briefly until fluffy. Add a little more milk if the mixture looks too dry.

Roasted: Peel or scrub and cut into even-sized pieces. Place in a pan and just cover with water. Add a little salt, part-cover with a lid, bring to the boil and cook for 3–4 minutes. Drain off the water. Cover firmly with the lid and, holding the lid on, give the pan a really good shake to roughen the edges of the potatoes. Meanwhile, heat a little oil in a roasting tin (baking pan) in the oven until sizzling. Add the potatoes (careful – they will spit). Turn over in the oil, then roast at the top of the oven at 190°C/375°F/gas mark 5 for about 1 hour, turning once or twice during the cooking time, until crisp and golden.

Sautéed: Cut into small pieces or dice. Heat a little oil (or half margarine, half oil) in a frying pan (skillet) and fry, turning, until golden brown and cooked through – about 7 minutes, depending on the size. Add a little garlic towards the end of cooking, if liked. Drain on kitchen paper before serving. Courgettes (zucchini) are great cooked this way too.

Carrots and other root vegetables

Boiled: Peel or scrub, then slice or cut into fingers. Cook as for potatoes (page 12) for 4–6 minutes or until tender.

Roasted: Prepare and cook as for potatoes (see above) but there's no need to shake the pan after par-boiling.

Green vegetables

Boiled: Shred or tear leafy ones, separate broccoli or cauliflower into small florets, top and tail beans or mangetout (snow peas) (and slice for runner beans), shell peas or broad (lima) beans. Drop into a very little boiling, lightly salted water, cover and boil rapidly until just tender, no longer. Drain (use the liquid for gravy or sauce if possible) and serve.

Steamed: Prepare as above but place in a colander over a pan of boiling water. Cover with a lid and steam until just tender. Don't put too many in the colander at one time, and allow a little longer than for boiling. Don't overcook or they will lose their colour and nutrients.

Rice

Boiled: Rinse and drain the rice. Bring a large pan of lightly salted water to the boil, add the rice, stir, then boil rapidly for 10–15 minutes until the rice is tender but the grains are still separate. Strain in a colander and pour some boiling water over to rinse off any excess starch and drain again.

TIPS: Allow 50 g/2 oz/¼ cup uncooked rice for an average serving. If using the rice cold, pour cold water over it to cool it quickly.

Oven-baked: Use 1 part rice to 2½ parts salted water or stock. Melt a knob of margarine in a flameproof casserole (Dutch oven). Add the rice and stir to coat. Add stock or water and bring to the boil. Cover and place in the oven at 180°C/350°F/gas mark 4. Cook for 20 minutes or until the rice is tender and has absorbed all the liquid. Don't overcook or it will go mushy.

Steamed: Use the same quantities as for oven-baked rice. Rinse and place the rice in a pan. Cover with the liquid and bring just to the boil. Cover with a piece of foil, then a tight-fitting lid. Turn down the heat as low as possible and cook for 15 minutes. DO NOT UNCOVER. Turn off the heat and leave to stand for 5 minutes (no more), then remove the cover and fluff up with a fork.

Pasta

Bring plenty of lightly salted water to the boil. Add the pasta and bring back to the boil. Add 15 ml/1 tbsp oil to prevent it boiling over, then boil rapidly for 10 minutes (or according to the packet directions), stirring occasionally to prevent sticking, until the pasta is just tender but still with a little 'bite'. Drain and use as required.

TIPS: Allow 50 g/2 oz/¼ cup uncooked pasta for an average serving. For spaghetti, bring the water to the boil, then stand the spaghetti in the water and gently push down so the spaghetti curls round in the pan as it softens in the boiling water.

Stir-frying

This is a way of cooking ingredients quickly to retain their flavour, texture and goodness. Cut vegetables and meat into strips as near the same size as possible to ensure even cooking. Heat a little oil in a wok or frying pan (skillet) until really hot. Add the ingredients carefully. They should start to cook immediately. Keep stirring all the time for a few minutes until cooked through.

Basic food hygiene

You may think some of the following are stating the obvious, but if you don't prepare, cook and store your food properly you're liable to get some pretty unpleasant side-effects!

Preparing food

★ Always wash your hands before preparing food
★ Don't lick your fingers
★ Keep work surfaces and cooker clean and free from spills and debris
★ Don't use a cloth to wipe down a chopping board you've been cutting raw meat on, for instance, then use the same one to wipe the surfaces – you'll simply spread germs. Always wash your cloth well in hot soapy water. Better still, use an antibacterial kitchen cleaner to wipe all surfaces
★ Always wash up in hot, soapy water and leave to drain rather than dry up with a manky tea towel
★ Keep the floor swept and washed or you might invite unwanted visitors such as mice to move in!
★ Don't leave dirty dishes festering in the kitchen (or anywhere else!)
★ Empty rubbish regularly

Storing food

★ Keep all perishables in the fridge
★ NEVER put raw and cooked meats or fish on the same shelf and always keep them covered. Always have raw meat on the bottom shelf, so no drips can contaminate other food, and always have it in or on a container to avoid leakages

★ Any half-used canned food should always be transferred to a container with a lid, not left in the fridge in the can

★ Always cool leftovers quickly by transferring them from their hot cooking container into a clean cold one. Cover loosely and as soon as they're cold put them in the fridge, properly covered. But do wait until they're cold – hot food in the fridge raises the temperature and can make it unsafe for all the food in it

★ NEVER leave cooked food on the stove or in the oven overnight – the warm surroundings are the perfect breeding ground for bacteria

★ NEVER leave food uncovered in the kitchen overnight. Any 'little friends' (and I don't mean your flatmates!) could have a snack while you're asleep!

★ Always eat food by its use-by date (not the sell-by date). If you buy fresh meat, fish or poultry on its sell-by date (it's often reduced then) but you're not going to use by the use-by date, freeze it immediately. When ready to cook it, make sure you thaw and use immediately. As soon as it is thawed, it is the same as it was the day you bought it. ALWAYS check the packaging to make sure food has not been previously frozen. If it has, you must eat it on the day of purchase

★ Don't keep leftovers festering in the fridge for days or weeks on end. As a rule of thumb, three days is about the limit for most things. Taste and smell are often a good guide to the state of your food. Anything that looks, smells or tastes off, is off!

★ Don't refreeze foods that have defrosted unless you cook them first

Cooking properly
★ NEVER reheat foods more than once and ALWAYS make sure any reheated food is piping hot right through. Eat it lukewarm and you're asking for trouble

★ ALWAYS make sure frozen meat is thoroughly thawed before cooking, especially poultry

★ Check any food is thoroughly cooked through before serving

★ With prepared frozen foods, check the packet directions to see if they should be cooked from frozen or thawed first

★ Don't keep tasting and stirring with the same spoon. I know they do it in the movies, but imagine, all that slobber going to be dished out to everyone – UGH!

NOTES ON THE RECIPES

★ All ingredients are in metric, Imperial and American measures. Use only one set per recipe and don't mix them up.

★ All eggs are medium unless otherwise stated.

★ All spoon measures are level. 1 tsp = 5 ml, 1 tbsp = 15 ml.

★ All can sizes are approximate – they differ slightly from brand to brand. For example, if I call for a 400 g/14 oz can of tomatoes, yours might be a 413 g can – that's fine.

★ Wash and peel, if necessary, all fresh produce before using.

★ All preparation and cooking times are approximate.

★ Always preheat the oven and cook on the centre shelf unless otherwise stated.

★ Most recipes serve at least two people, so if you're eating alone have it on two days. You can in most cases halve the quantities if you like, but it's just as quick to cook enough for two meals in one go!

★ Occasionally where cans are among the ingredients I have given a recipe for 4 people, so that you don't have a lot of half-used cans hanging around in the fridge.

SNACKS AND ULTRA-EASY MEALS

FEED ME

Any of the recipes in this section make perfect light lunches or suppers on their own. But equally they can become your main meal with extra salad, bread or spuds.

TIP: If money is seriously running out, bread, cheese and any salad bits make a very nutritious meal and any of the ideas on the following pages make good filling fodder.

Stuffed jacket potatoes: bake them (see page 13), split in half and scoop out the potato into a bowl. Mash with a little margarine and add any of the following:
★ Sweetcorn (corn) and grated cheese
★ Baked beans and grated cheese
★ Tuna, chopped cucumber and mayonnaise
★ Chopped ham (even a scrap) and cheese
★ Marmite (Vegemite) and grated cheese
★ Canned minced steak and onion

Plain boiled pasta: drain, then add any of the following, cooking and stirring gently until piping hot:
★ Knob of margarine and grated cheese
★ Chopped can of tomatoes, a few dried herbs and grated cheese
★ Drained can of peas, a knob of margarine and a little grated cheese
★ Egg beaten with a little milk, salt and pepper, a few mixed herbs and/or grated cheese
★ Egg beaten with a little milk, seasoning and a can of sweetcorn (corn)
★ Margarine, Marmite (Vegemite) and grated cheese
★ Peanut butter, a little milk and a pinch of chilli, with cheese too, if liked

Plain boiled rice: drain and add any of the following:
★ Drained can of red kidney beans, some chilli powder and grated cheese
★ Drained can of peas, a beaten egg and some soy or Worcestershire sauce
★ Chopped can of tomatoes, some dried herbs and a drained can of any beans
★ Drained can of tuna and some mayonnaise
★ Drained can of pineapple, tuna or beans and mayonnaise or soy sauce (good hot or cold)

FISH FINGERS AMERICAN-STYLE

Serves 2

Ingredients	Metric	Imperial	American
Fish fingers	8	8	8
Soft baps	2	2	2
Processed cheese slices	2	2	2
Ready-made tartare sauce OR mayonnaise	30 ml	2 tbsp	2 tbsp
Lettuce, shredded			

1. Cook the fish fingers according to the packet directions.

2. Split the baps and lay 4 fish fingers in each one.

3. Top with a slice of cheese and flash under a hot grill (broiler) to melt the cheese.

4. Top with tartare sauce or mayonnaise, shredded lettuce and then the lid of the bap.

Preparation time: 2 minutes
Cooking time: 8 minutes

PLOUGHMAN'S GRILL

Serves 2

Ingredients	Metric	Imperial	American
Slices of bread	2	2	2
Margarine	25 g	1 oz	2 tbsp
Cheddar cheese, grated	50 g	2 oz	½ cup
Pickled onions, chopped	2	2	2

1. **Toast the bread on both sides.**

2. **Meanwhile, mash the margarine with the cheese and pickled onions.**

3. **Spread over the toast and grill (broil) until golden and bubbling. Serve hot.**

Preparation time: 3 minutes
Cooking time: 4 minutes

SPICY POTATO CAKES

Serves 2

Ingredients	Metric	Imperial	American
Large potatoes, grated	2	2	2
Small onion, grated	1	1	1
Garam masala	2.5 ml	½ tsp	½ tsp
Chilli powder	1.5 ml	¼ tsp	¼ tsp
Egg, beaten	1	1	1
Plain (all-purpose) flour	5 ml	1 tsp	1 tsp
Salt and pepper			
Oil	30 ml	2 tbsp	2 tbsp
To serve: Mango chutney			

1. Mix the potatoes, onion, spices, egg and flour together.

2. Heat the oil in a frying pan (skillet) and fry (sauté) the mixture a tablespoonful at a time until golden brown underneath. Turn over and fry the other side for 4–5 minutes in all.

3. Serve hot with mango chutney.

Preparation time: 5–8 minutes
Cooking time: 5 minutes

TIP: You can use curry powder instead of garam masala and chilli powder if you prefer.

PITTA POCKETS

Serves 1–2

Ingredients	Metric	Imperial	American
Pitta bread	2	2	2
Lettuce, shredded			
Tomato, sliced	1	1	1
Cucumber slices	4	4	4

For the filling:

Tuna, chopped ham, mashed pilchards, sliced corned beef, chopped frankfurter, salami, hard-boiled (hard-cooked) egg, mayonnaise

1. **Toast or microwave the pittas just to heat through enough to puff up. Split along one long edge to form a pocket.**

2. **Add shredded lettuce, tomato, cucumber and one of the suggested fillings. Finish with mayonnaise.**

Preparation time: 2 minutes
Cooking time: nil

NAN TIFFIN

Serves 2

Ingredients	Metric	Imperial	American
Naan bread	2	2	2
Can of pease pudding	225 g	8 oz	1 small
Curry paste	10 ml	2 tsp	2 tsp
Mango chutney	30 ml	2 tbsp	2 tbsp
Lemon juice (optional)			
Lettuce, shredded (optional)			

1. **Grill or microwave the naan bread according to the packet directions.**

2. **Heat the pease pudding with the curry paste in a saucepan until hot, stirring occasionally.**

3. **Spread the pease pudding mixture over the surface of the naan bread.**

4. **Spread with mango chutney and sprinkle with lemon juice, if using. Add the shredded lettuce, if liked.**

5. **Fold in half, then cut into manageable wedges.**

6. **Wrap in kitchen paper and eat in your fingers.**

Preparation time: 2 minutes
Cooking time: 3 minutes

MELTING CRESCENTS

As an alternative you can spread the croissant with soft garlic and herb cheese and add some chopped red (bell) pepper before grilling.

Serves 1

Ingredients	Metric	Imperial	American
Croissant	1	1	1
Salami slices	2	2	2
OR ham slice	1	1	1
Processed cheese slice	1	1	1

To serve: Tomato slices

1. Split the croissant almost in half and fill with the folded salami or ham and cheese slices.

2. Place under a moderate grill (broiler) until the cheese melts, turning once. Take care not to let it burn.

Preparation time: 2 minutes
Cooking time: 3 minutes

CHEESE AND MUSHROOM CROISSANTS

Serves 4

Ingredients	Metric	Imperial	American
Croissants	4	4	4
Can of creamed mushrooms	215 g	7½ oz	1 small
Cheddar cheese, grated	50 g	2 oz	½ cup

1. **Carefully split open the croissants without breaking them apart.**

2. **Spread the creamed mushrooms inside and pack in the cheese.**

3. **Grill (broil), turning once, until the cheese has melted and the croissants are crisp and hot through. Take care not to let them burn. Alternatively heat as for Pizza Rolls (see page 31).**

 Preparation time: 2 minutes
Cooking time: 5 minutes

EGGY BAGUETTE

Serves 1–2

Ingredients	Metric	Imperial	American
Small French stick	1	1	1
Margarine			
Eggs	2	2	2
Dried mixed herbs	1.5 ml	¼ tsp	¼ tsp
Salt and pepper			

1. **Warm the French stick either in the oven or under the grill (broiler), turning frequently. Cut a slit along the length and spread with margarine.**

2. **Meanwhile, beat the eggs and add 30 ml/2 tbsp water, the herbs and some salt and pepper. Beat well.**

3. **Heat a frying pan (skillet) and add a knob of margarine. When sizzling pour in the egg mixture. Lift and stir in the egg until set.**

4. **Fold the omelette, slide inside the French stick and cut in half, if liked.**

Preparation time: 5 minutes
Cooking time: about 8 minutes

WAFFLE DAGWOODS

Serves 2

Ingredients	Metric	Imperial	American
Frozen potato waffles	4	4	4
Eggs	2	2	2
Oil			
Ham slices	2	2	2
Lettuce, shredded			

1. Gril (broil) or fry (sauté) the waffles according to the packet directions.

2. Fry (sauté) the eggs in a little oil until cooked.

3. Place each slice of ham on a waffle. Top both with an egg and some shredded lettuce. Finish with a second waffle – and try to eat!

Preparation time: 2 minutes
Cooking time: about 6 minutes

CROQUE MADAME
A smart fried sandwich!

Serves 1

Ingredients	Metric	Imperial	American
Slices of bread	2	2	2
Margarine			
Processed cheese slice	1	1	1
Onion, sliced and separated into rings	1	1	1
Dried sage	1.5 ml	¼ tsp	¼ tsp

1. **Spread the bread with the margarine. Sandwich together with the cheese, onion rings and sage, 'buttered' sides out.**

2. **Fry (sauté) in a frying pan (skillet) on each side for about 2 minutes or until golden and the cheese has melted.**

3. **Serve immediately.**

Preparation time: 2 minutes
Cooking time: about 4 minutes

Variation: Croque Monsieur – another smart fried sandwich! Prepare as for Croque Madame but substitute the sliced onions with a slice of ham. Omit the sage.

PIZZA ROLLS

Serves 2–4

Ingredients	Metric	Imperial	American
Soft rolls	4	4	4
Can of tomatoes, drained	227 g	8 oz	1 small
Dried oregano	5 ml	1 tsp	1 tsp
Mozzarella or Cheddar cheese, grated			

1. Cut a slit in the top of each roll, not quite through.

2. Gently pull away some of the soft filling to leave a thick shell.

3. Chop the tomatoes. Divide between the rolls, sprinkle with herbs and top with cheese.

4. Wrap each roll in foil and steam in a colander over a saucepan of boiling water for 10 minutes until the cheese has melted. Alternatively, bake in a preheated oven at 220°C/425°F/gas mark 7 for 10 minutes.

Preparation time: 3 minutes
Cooking time: 10 minutes

TIP: You can always make up the 4 rolls and keep 2 in the fridge to heat up another day.

OMELETTE IN THE FINGERS

Serves 2

Ingredients	Metric	Imperial	American
Eggs	4	4	4
Cold water	60 ml	4 tbsp	4 tbsp
Salt and pepper			
Dried mixed herbs	5 ml	1 tsp	1 tsp
Can of whole green beans, drained	298 g	10½ oz	1 small

To serve: Crusty bread and chunky salad pieces

1. Beat 1 egg into a bowl with 15 ml/1 tbsp of water, a little salt and pepper and 1.5 ml/¼ tsp herbs.

2. Heat a little margarine in a frying pan (skillet). Pour in the egg and fry (sauté), lifting the edge and letting uncooked egg run underneath until set. Transfer to a plate and leave to cool while making 3 more omelettes in the same way.

3. Divide the beans between the omelettes.

4. Roll up and serve with crusty bread and chunky salad pieces that can be eaten in the fingers.

Preparation time: 2 minutes
Cooking time: about 10 minutes, plus cooling

TUNA DIP

Serves 2

Ingredients	Metric	Imperial	American
Can of tuna, drained	185 g	6½ oz	1 small
Mayonnaise	60 ml	4 tbsp	4 tbsp
Plain yoghurt	45 ml	3 tbsp	3 tbsp
Tomato ketchup (catsup)	15 ml	1 tbsp	1 tbsp
Vinegar or lemon juice	5 ml	1 tsp	1 tsp
Chilli powder	1.5 ml	¼ tsp	¼ tsp
Pepper			

To serve: Vegetable 'dippers' and fingers of crisp toast

1. **Put the tuna in a bowl and break up with a wooden spoon. Beat in the remaining ingredients until well blended.**

2. **Serve with vegetable 'dippers' such as small florets of cauliflower, sticks of cucumber, carrot and green or red (bell) pepper and fingers of crisp toast.**

 **Preparation time: 3 minutes
Cooking time: nil**

TUNA CHEESE

Serves 1

Ingredients	Metric	Imperial	American
Can of tuna, drained	85 g	3½ oz	1 very small
Low-fat soft cheese	100 g	4 oz	½ cup
Vinegar or lemon juice	5 ml	1 tsp	1 tsp
Pinch of cayenne or chilli powder			
Salt and pepper			
Cucumber, diced	¼	¼	¼
To serve: Hot toast and tomato wedges			

1. **Mash the tuna in a bowl with the cheese.**

2. **Add the remaining ingredients and mix well.**

3. **Serve with hot toast and tomato wedges.**

Preparation time: 5 minutes
Cooking time: nil

SPICY SARDINE AND BEAN PITTAS

Serves 2

Ingredients	Metric	Imperial	American
Can of sardines or pilchards in tomato sauce	120 g	4½ oz	1 small
Garlic purée (paste)	1.5 ml	¼ tsp	¼ tsp
Chilli powder	1.5 ml	¼ tsp	¼ tsp
Can of butter beans, drained and mashed	213 g	7½ oz	1 small
Salt and pepper			
Wholemeal pitta breads	4	4	4
Lettuce, shredded			
Cucumber slices			

1. Mash the sardines or pilchards, preferably including the bones.

2. Add the garlic purée, chilli and mashed beans and season to taste.

3. Grill (broil) the pittas briefly until they begin to puff up.

4. Make a slit along one side of each to form a pocket.

5. Spoon in the sardine mixture and add some shredded lettuce and cucumber slices.

 Preparation time: 4 minutes
Cooking time: nil

EGGY BREAD

Serves 1–2

Ingredients	Metric	Imperial	American
Eggs	2	2	2
Dash of milk			
Salt and pepper			
Slices of bread	3	3	3
Oil			

1. Beat the eggs with the milk and a little salt and pepper.

2. Cut each slice of bread into quarters and dip into the egg mixture until completely coated.

3. Heat the oil and fry (sauté) the soaked bread until golden brown on both sides. Sprinkle with salt and pepper and serve hot.

 Preparation time: 4 minutes
Cooking time: 3–4 minutes

HASH BROWNS

Serves 2

Ingredients	Metric	Imperial	American
Oil	45 ml	3 tbsp	3 tbsp
Potatoes, finely diced	450 g	1 lb	1 lb
Onion, chopped	1	1	1
Salt and pepper			

To serve: Fried eggs (see page 12)

1. Heat the oil and fry (sauté) the potato over a low heat for 10 minutes until soft. Remove from the pan with a slotted spoon.

2. Add the potatoes to the pan and fry, turning, until golden on the outside and soft inside – about 10 minutes. Add the onions to the pan, season well with salt and pepper and cook for a further 5 minutes until the mixture is soft and brown. Press down firmly to form a 'cake'.

3. Divide in half and serve topped with fried eggs.

Preparation time: 6 minutes
Cooking time: 15 minutes

SOMERSET RAREBIT

You can substitute beer or white wine for the cider.
Make double the quantity for a quick cheese fondue to
serve with cubes of French bread.

Serves 1 or 2

Ingredients	Metric	Imperial	American
Cheddar cheese, grated	175 g	6 oz	1½ cups
Mustard	5 ml	1 tsp	1 tsp
Cider	30 ml	2 tbsp	2 tbsp
Slices of toast	2	2	2

1. Put all the ingredients except the toast in a small pan.
   Heat gently, stirring, until the cheese has melted and the
   mixture is well blended.

2. Spoon on to toast and serve.

Preparation time: 5 minutes
Cooking time: about 5 minutes

DEVILLED MUSHROOMS

Serves 2

Ingredients	Metric	Imperial	American
Small onion, finely chopped	1	1	1
Oil	15 ml	1 tbsp	1 tbsp
Button mushrooms	175 g	6 oz	6 oz
Tomatoes, chopped	2	2	2
Tomato ketchup (catsup)	10 ml	2 tsp	2 tsp
Worcestershire sauce	10 ml	2 tsp	2 tsp
Tabasco sauce	1–2 drops	1–2 drops	1–2 drops
Pinch of chilli powder			
To serve: Hot buttered toast			

I. **Cook the onion in the oil for 2 minutes until softened. Add the mushrooms and tomatoes and cook, stirring, for 2 minutes.**

2. **Add the remaining ingredients and simmer for about 5 minutes or until the mushrooms are just cooked.**

3. **Serve on hot buttered toast.**

Preparation time: 5 minutes
Cooking time: 9 minutes

TIP: Turn this into a substantial main meal by adding a drained 430 g/15½ oz can of chick peas (garbanzos) at step 2. Serve with lots of crusty bread and a green salad instead of on toast.

GARLIC BREAD

Serve as a snack or with any soups or main courses.
It's lovely served with a hunk of cheese and tomatoes
for a posh Ploughman's!

Serves 6

Ingredients	Metric	Imperial	American
Margarine	100 g	4 oz	½ cup
Garlic purée (paste)	10 ml	2 tsp	2 tsp
Small French stick	1	1	1

1. **Blend together the margarine and the garlic purée.**

2. **Cut the French stick into 12 slices, not quite slicing through the bottom crust to keep the loaf intact.**

3. **Spread the garlic mixture between the slices and over the top. Wrap in foil, shiny side in, and bake in a preheated oven at 200°C/400°F/gas mark 6 for about 15 minutes until the crust feels crisp but the centre is still soft.**

Preparation time: 5–10 minutes
Cooking time: 15 minutes

Variation: Garlic Rolls
Spread the garlic mixture in 6 white or wholemeal rolls or bagels. Wrap in foil and bake as above or grill (broil) for 15 minutes, turning once.

HERB BREAD

Serves 6

Ingredients	Metric	Imperial	American
Margarine	100 g	4 oz	½ cup
Dried mixed herbs	10 ml	2 tsp	2 tsp
Salt and pepper			
Small French stick	1	1	1

1. **Blend the margarine and dried herbs together, seasoning generously with salt and pepper.**

2. **Cut the French stick into 12 slices, not quite slicing through the bottom crust to keep the loaf intact.**

3. **Spread the herb mixture between the slices and over the top. Wrap in foil, shiny side in, and bake in a preheated oven at 200°C/400°F/gas mark 6 for about 15 minutes until the crust feels crisp but the centre is still soft.**

**Preparation time: 5–10 minutes
Cooking time: 15 minutes**

TIP: Add a squeeze of lemon juice and some chopped fresh parsley for a special flavour.

MEATLESS MEALS

FEED ME

As meat is so costly, you may find having vegetarian-style food is a good, cheap option some of the time. All the following dishes are highly nutritious and very economical, using pulses, cheese or eggs for protein. If you're cooking for serious vegetarians, make sure any cheese you use is suitable (read the labels). I've used canned dried beans for quickness and many supermarket own brands and less well-known makes are very cheap.

I haven't used Quorn or tofu in this book as they are comparatively expensive. But if you want to use minced Quorn, for instance, simply substitute it for any of the mince recipes in the Other Meaty Meals chapter. You'll need to add a little oil when frying (sautéing) it with the onion during preparation. Cubes of tofu would make a tasty substitute for some of the fish dishes in this book.

TIP: If you want to make mega savings, buy a packet of dried beans, soak them in cold water, then boil rapidly for 10 minutes, reduce the heat and simmer for at least 1 hour, depending on the type, until they are tender. Don't add salt or you'll toughen them. Top up with more boiling water during cooking if necessary. Once cooked, drain and store in a covered container in the fridge for several days to use as required, or pack in plastic bags in usable amounts. (A 450 g/1 lb pack of dried beans is the equivalent of 4 × 425 g/15 oz cans.)

NO-SWEAT VEGGIE SOUP

Serves 2–4, depending on the quantities used

Ingredients	Metric	Imperial	American
Use whatever vegetables you have to hand: carrots, potatoes, outer leaves of cabbage, parsnips, beans, peas, onions – anything.			
Stock cubes			
Dried mixed herbs			
Salt and pepper			
To serve: Grated cheese and crusty bread			

I. **Dice, grate or shred your choice of vegetables and place in a saucepan. Cover with water and add a couple of stock cubes. Sprinkle a few dried mixed herbs over the surface. Bring to the boil, part-cover with a lid and simmer for about 10–15 minutes, until all the vegetables are soft.**

2. **Season to taste and serve with loads of grated cheese and crusty bread.**

Preparation time: about 10 minutes
Cooking time: 10–15 minutes

TIP: To make this soup even more filling and nutritious, add a can of any sort of pulse (beans or lentils) or a can of sweetcorn (corn).

PEANUT SOUP

This recipe is so easy, you might as well make enough for 2 days.

Serves 4–6

Ingredients	Metric	Imperial	American
Small onion, grated	1	1	1
Carrot, grated	1	1	1
Margarine	25 g	1 oz	2 tbsp
Plain (all-purpose) flour	20 g	¾ oz	3 tbsp
Chicken stock, made with 2 stock cubes	1 litre	1¾ pts	4¼ cups
Smooth peanut butter	225 g	8 oz	1 cup
Single (light) cream or milk	200 ml	7 fl oz	scant 1 cup
To serve: Crusty bread			

1. **Fry (sauté) the onion and carrot in the margarine in a pan for 2 minutes, stirring.**

2. **Sprinkle in the flour and cook, stirring, for 1 minute. Remove from the heat.**

3. **Gradually blend in the stock. Return to the heat, bring to the boil, stirring, and simmer for 5 minutes.**

4. **Blend in the peanut butter and cream or milk. Reheat, but do not boil.**

5. **Serve in soups bowls or mugs and accompany with lots of crusty bread.**

Preparation time: 5 minutes
Cooking time: 8–10 minutes

RICE AND SPINACH SOUP

Serves 2

Ingredients	Metric	Imperial	American
Frozen chopped spinach, thawed	150 g	5 oz	5 oz
Chicken or vegetable stock, made with 1 stock cube	600 ml	1 pt	2½ cups
Knob of margarine			
Long-grain rice	50 g	2 oz	¼ cup
Salt and pepper			
To serve: Grated Parmesan or Cheddar cheese			

I. **Place the spinach in a pan with the stock and the margarine. Bring to the boil.**

2. **Add the rice, reduce the heat and simmer for 15–20 minutes, until the rice is just tender.**

3. **Season to taste, ladle into soup bowls or mugs and serve with lots of grated cheese.**

Preparation time: 3 minutes
Cooking time: 15–20 minutes

CUBAN EGGS

Serves 2

Ingredients	Metric	Imperial	American
Long-grain rice	100 g	4 oz	½ cup
Small onion, finely chopped	1	1	1
Garlic purée (paste)	1.5 ml	¼ tsp	¼ tsp
Oil	60 ml	4 tbsp	4 tbsp
Banana, cut into thick chunks	1	1	1
Eggs	2	2	2

1. Cook the rice in plenty of boiling salted water for 10 minutes or until tender. Drain.

2. Meanwhile, fry (sauté) the onion and garlic purée in 15 m/1 tbsp of the oil until soft and brown. Remove from the pan with a draining spoon and keep warm.

3. Add a further 15 ml/1 tbsp of the oil to the pan and fry the bananas until just cooked but still holding their shape. Add to the onion.

4. Heat the remaining oil and fry the eggs until set.

5. Pile the rice on 2 warm plates. Slide an egg on top of each and serve with the fried onion and garlic and the banana chunks.

Preparation time: 5 minutes
Cooking time: 14 minutes

WINTER RIB-STICKER

Serves 2

Ingredients	Metric	Imperial	American
Red lentils	50 g	2 oz	⅓ cup
Water	600 ml	1 pt	2½ cups
Leek, chopped	1	1	1
Potato, chopped	1	1	1
Carrot, chopped	1	1	1
Small parsnip, chopped	1	1	1
Small turnip, chopped	1	1	1
Small swede (rutabaga), chopped	½	½	½
Vegetable stock cube	½	½	½
Salt and pepper			

1. **Place the lentils in a large pan with the water. Bring to the boil, then skim off any scum.**

2. **Add the vegetables and stock cube.**

3. **Return to the boil, then simmer for about 20 minutes, stirring occasionally, until the soup is thick and the vegetables soft. Season to taste.**

Preparation time: 10 minutes
Cooking time: 20 minutes

EGG AND VEGETABLE PLATTER

Use 4 eggs if you're really hungry, 2 if you just want a light meal.

Serves 2

Ingredients	Metric	Imperial	American
Cooked left-over vegetables including potatoes OR cooked frozen vegetables and a little prepared instant mash	225 g	8 oz	2 cups
Pepper			
Knob of margarine			
Brown table sauce	15 ml	1 tbsp	1 tbsp
Eggs	2 or 4	2 or 4	2 or 4
Oil			

1. Chop the vegetables. Season lightly with pepper. Melt the margarine in a large frying pan (skillet) and add half the vegetables. Press down flat.

2. Spread the brown sauce over the top with the rest of the vegetables, and press down well again.

3. Cover with a plate and cook gently for about 15 minutes. Then loosen the base and turn out on to a plate. Cut in half.

4. Meanwhile fry the eggs in a little oil (or poach in water). Slide the eggs on top of the vegetable cake and serve.

Preparation time: 3 minutes
Cooking time: 15 minutes

BASIC MACARONI CHEESE

Serves 2 or 3

Ingredients	Metric	Imperial	American
Short-cut macaroni	100 g	4 oz	4 oz
Plain (all-purpose) flour	25 g	1 oz	¼ cup
Milk	300 ml	½ pt	1 ¼ cups
Margarine	25 g	1 oz	2 tbsp
Mustard	5 ml	1 tsp	1 tsp
Cheddar cheese, grated	75 g	3 oz	¾ cup
Salt and pepper			
Extra grated cheese (optional)			

1. Cook the macaroni according to the packet directions. Drain.

2. Whisk the flour with a little of the milk in a saucepan until smooth. Whisk in the remaining milk and add the margarine. Bring to the boil and boil for 2 minutes, stirring all the time.

3. Stir in the mustard and cheese and season to taste with salt and pepper. Add to the pasta and stir well.

4. Either spoon on to plates or turn into a flameproof dish, top with a little extra grated cheese and grill (broil) until golden and bubbling.

 Preparation time: 5 minutes
Cooking time: 20–25 minutes

MAKESHIFT MULLIGATAWNY

Serves 2–4

Ingredients	Metric	Imperial	American
Cooked leftover mixed vegetables (or use frozen)	225 g	8 oz	2 cups
Garlic purée (paste)	1.5 ml	¼ tsp	¼ tsp
Curry paste	5–10 ml	1–2 tsp	1–2 tsp
Oil	15 ml	1 tbsp	1 tbsp
Vegetable stock, made with 1 stock cube	600 ml	1 pt	2½ cups
Tomato purée (paste)	15 ml	1 tbsp	1 tbsp
Instant mashed potato powder (optional)	15 ml	1 tbsp	1 tbsp
Salt and pepper			

To garnish (when friends come): Slices of lemon

1. **Fry (sauté) the vegetables, garlic purée and curry paste in the oil for 1 minute.**

2. **Add the stock and tomato purée, bring to the boil and simmer for 5 minutes.**

3. **Thicken, if liked, by sprinkling the mashed potato powder over, then stirring it in. Season to taste. Reheat.**

4. **Serve in warm soup bowls with a slice of lemon on top, if liked.**

Preparation time: 2 minutes
Cooking time: 7 minutes

EGG AND MACARONI POPEYE-STYLE

Serves 3

Ingredients	Metric	Imperial	American
1 quantity of Basic Macaroni Cheese (see page 49)			
Chopped frozen spinach	350 g	12 oz	12 oz
Hard boiled (hard-cooked) eggs	2 or 3	2 or 3	2 or 3

I. Cook the macaroni and cheese sauce as for Basic Macaroni Cheese, but do not mix together.

2. Cook the spinach according to the packet directions. Drain thoroughly and place in the bottom of an ovenproof dish.

3. Cover the spinach with the macaroni, then the eggs.

4. Spoon the cheese sauce over the top and bake in a preheated oven at 190°C/375°F/gas mark 5 for 25–30 minutes until bubbling and golden.

Preparation time: 20 minutes
Cooking time: 20–25 minutes

Variation: For Rosy Eggs with Macaroni, prepare as above but substitute 440 g/14 oz/1 large can of tomatoes, chopped, for the spinach.

SPECIAL MACARONI CHEESE

Serves 2 or 3

Ingredients	Metric	Imperial	American
Short-cut macaroni	100 g	4 oz	4 oz
Mushrooms, sliced	50 g	2 oz	2 oz
Green (bell) pepper, diced	½	½	½
Plain (all-purpose) flour	25 g	1 oz	¼ cup
Milk	300 ml	½ pt	1¼ cups
Margarine	50 g	2 oz	¼ cup
Mustard	5 ml	1 tsp	1 tsp
Cheddar cheese, grated	75 g	3 oz	¾ cup
Salt and pepper			
Tomato, sliced	1	1	1
Extra grated cheese			

1. Cook the macaroni according to the packet directions. Drain.

2. Meanwhile, fry (sauté) the mushrooms and pepper in half the margarine, drain and keep warm.

3. Whisk the flour with a little of the milk in a saucepan until smooth. Whisk in the remaining milk and add the rest of the margarine. Bring to the boil and boil for 2 minutes, stirring all the time.

4. Stir in the mustard and cheese and season to taste with salt and pepper. Add to the pasta, mushrooms and peppers and stir well.

5. Turn into a flameproof dish. Arrange the tomato slices on top and cover with a little extra grated cheese. Grill (broil) until golden and bubbling.

Preparation time: 5 minutes
Cooking time: 20–25 minutes

TIP: For non-vegetarians, stir in 50 g/2 oz of diced cooked ham when you add the pasta.

SAVOURY EGGS RICE

Serves 2

Ingredients	Metric	Imperial	American
Packet of savoury rice (any flavour)	1	1	1
Eggs	4	4	4
To serve: Garlic bread (see page 40)			

I. Empty the packet of rice into a large frying pan (skillet). Add water as directed on the packet and bring to the boil. Cover with a lid and simmer for 15 minutes.

2. Remove the lid stir, make 4 'wells' in the rice mixture, break an egg into each, cover and continue cooking over a gentle heat for 5 minutes or until the eggs are set.

3. Serve straight from the pan with garlic bread.

Preparation time: 2 minutes
Cooking time: 20 minutes

MUSHROOM AND NUT PILAF

Serves 2

Ingredients	Metric	Imperial	American
Long-grain rice	100 g	4 oz	½ cup
Small onion, sliced	1	1	1
Oil	15 ml	1 tbsp	1 tbsp
Garlic purée (paste)	2.5 ml	½ tsp	½ tsp
Button mushrooms, sliced	100	4 oz	4 oz
Green (bell) pepper	1	1	1
Peanuts and raisins	50 g	2 oz	½ cup
Soy sauce			

I. **Cook the rice in plenty of boiling salted water for 10 minutes or until tender. Drain.**

2. **Meanwhile, fry (sauté) the onion, garlic purée, mushrooms, pepper, peanuts and raisins.**

3. **Add the rice and soy sauce to taste, remembering that it is very salty. Fry for 2–3 minutes until heated through.**

Preparation time: 6 minutes
Cooking time: 12–13 minutes

OVEN OMELETTE

Serves 1–2

Ingredients	Metric	Imperial	American
Eggs, beaten	2	2	2
Cottage cheese	100 g	4 oz	½ cup
Milk	75 ml	5 tbsp	5 tbsp
Salt and pepper			
Button mushrooms, sliced	50 g	2 oz	2 oz
Small onion, chopped	1	1	1
Dried mixed herbs	pinch	pinch	pinch
To serve: Salad roll or sandwich			

1. **Mix all the ingredients in a bowl.**

2. **Pour into a well-greased ovenproof dish.**

3. **Bake in a preheated oven at 200°C/400°F/gas mark 6 for 15–20 minutes until brown and firm.**

4. **Serve cut into wedges, with a salad roll or sandwich.**

 Preparation time: 3 minutes
Cooking time: 20 minutes

FRENCH OMELETTE

Serves 1

Ingredients	Metric	Imperial	American
Eggs	2	2	2
Dried mixed herbs	1.5 ml	¼ tsp	¼ tsp
Milk	15 ml	1 tbsp	1 tbsp
Salt and pepper			
Oil			
Small onion, chopped	1	1	1
Brie or Camembert, sliced	50 g	2 oz	2 oz

To serve: Tomato and onion-filled piece of French bread

1. Beat together the eggs, herbs, milk and seasoning.

2. Heat a little oil in a frying pan (skillet) and lightly fry (sauté) the onion for 2 minutes.

3. Add the egg mixture and cook gently until almost set and firm underneath.

4. Lay the cheese over one half of the omelette, fold in half and press lightly. Cook for a further 1–2 minutes.

5. Serve straight away with a piece of French bread filled with tomato and onion.

Preparation time: 3 minutes
Cooking time: 5–7 minutes

CURRIED PARNSIP SOUP

This recipe is equally good made with sweet potatoes or yams instead of parsnips.

Serves 4

Ingredients	Metric	Imperial	American
Parsnips, sliced	450 g	1 lb	1 lb
Onion, chopped	1	1	1
Curry powder	15 ml	1 tbsp	1 tbsp
Margarine	25 g	1 oz	2 tbsp
Vegetable stock, made with 1 stock cube	600 ml	1 pt	2½ cups
Milk	300 ml	½ pt	1¼ cups
Salt and pepper			

To garnish (when friends come): Chopped parsley

1. Put the parsnips, onion, curry powder and margarine in a pan. Fry (sauté) gently, stirring, for 3 minutes.

2. Stir in the stock, bring to the boil, reduce the heat, cover and simmer for 15 minutes, or until the parsnips are really tender.

3. Mash with a potato masher.

4. Stir in the milk, season to taste and heat through.

5. Serve ladled into soup bowls garnished with parsley, if liked.

Preparation time: 10 minutes
Cooking time: 20 minutes

DHAL

Serves 2

Ingredients	Metric	Imperial	American
Red lentils	175 g	6 oz	1 cup
Onion, chopped	1	1	1
Garlic purée (paste)	5 ml	1 tsp	1 tsp
Curry powder	30 ml	2 tbsp	2 tbsp
Vegetable stock, made with 2 stock cubes	600 ml	1 pt	2½ cups

To serve: Naan bread OR rice with salad and chutney

1. **Put all the ingredients into a saucepan and bring to the boil.**

2. **Skim the surface, then simmer for 20–30 minutes until very mushy, stirring frequently to stop it sticking to the bottom of the pan. Add a little more water while cooking if the lentils become too dry.**

3. **Serve hot with naan bread or rice, salad and chutney.**

Preparation time: 4 minutes
Cooking time: 20–30 minutes

MIDDLE EASTERN COTTAGE CHEESE PASTA

Serves 2–3

Ingredients	Metric	Imperial	American
Pappardelle or tagliatelle	175 g	6 oz	6 oz
Knob of margarine			
Cottage cheese	450 g	1 lb	2 cups
Caraway seeds	25 g	1 oz	¼ cup
Poppy seeds	25 g	1 oz	¼ cup
Salt and pepper			
Chilli powder			
To serve: Green salad			

1. Cook the pasta according to the packet directions. Drain and toss in the margarine, then return to the pan.

2. Add the cottage cheese, seeds, a little salt and pepper and chilli powder to taste.

3. Toss over a gentle heat until heated through.

4. Serve straight away with a green salad.

Preparation time: 3 minutes
Cooking time: 12 minutes

FLUFFY CHEESE PUDDING

Serves 2

Ingredients	Metric	Imperial	American
Margarine	15 g	½ oz	1 tbsp
Egg, separated	1	1	1
Milk	150 ml	¼ pt	⅔ cup
Thick slices of bread, crusts removed	2	2	2
Cheddar cheese, grated	50 g	2 oz	½ cup
Salt and pepper			
To serve: Canned tomatoes			

1. Grease an ovenproof dish well with the margarine.

2. Beat the egg yolk with the milk in the greased dish and crumble in the bread. Add the cheese and a little salt and pepper. Leave to stand for 15 minutes.

3. Whisk the egg white until stiff and gently fold into the mixture with a metal spoon.

4. Cook in a preheated oven at 200°C/400°F/gas mark 6 for about 25 minutes until risen and golden.

5. Serve immediately with canned tomatoes.

Preparation time: 3 minutes, plus standing time
Cooking time: 25 minutes

MEGA MINESTRONE

Serves 4

Ingredients	Metric	Imperial	American
Small onion, grated	1	1	1
Oil	15 ml	1 tbsp	1 tbsp
Carrot, grated	1	1	1
Small parsnip or turnip, grated	1	1	1
Small cabbage, shredded	¼	¼	¼
Frozen peas	50 g	2 oz	½ cup
Quick-cook macaroni	25 g	1 oz	1 oz
Can of tomatoes	400 g	14 oz	1 large
Vegetable stock cube	1	1	1
Dried oregano or mixed herbs	2.5 ml	½ tsp	½ tsp
Salt and pepper			

To serve: Grated Parmesan or Cheddar cheese and crusty bread

1. **Fry (sauté) the onion in the oil in a large pan for 30 seconds, stirring.**

2. **Add the remaining ingredients with 2 canfuls of water. Break up the tomatoes with a wooden spoon.**

3. **Bring to the boil, reduce the heat and simmer for 10 minutes, or until the vegetables and pasta are soft. Taste and adjust the seasoning if necessary.**

4. **Serve in soup bowls with cheese to sprinkle over and crusty bread.**

Preparation time: 10 minutes
Cooking time: 10 minutes

BEAN STEW WITH DUMPLINGS

This is excellent reheated the next day.

Serves 4 (or 2 and 2)

Ingredients	Metric	Imperial	American
Can of tomatoes	400 g	14 oz	1 large
Can of butter beans, drained	425 g	15 oz	1 large
Can of black-eyed beans, drained	425 g	15 oz	1 large
Garlic purée (paste)	2.5 ml	½ tsp	½ tsp
Tomato purée (paste)	15 ml	1 tbsp	1 tbsp
Can of sweetcorn (corn) with (bell) peppers	200 g	7 oz	1 small
Can of cut green beans	278 g	10 oz	1 small
Vegetable stock (made with 1 stock cube)	300 ml	½ pt	1¼ cups
Dried mixed herbs	2.5 ml	½ tsp	½ tsp
Salt and pepper			
Packet of dumpling mix	1	1	1
Cheddar cheese, grated	50 g	2 oz	½ cup

1. **Empty the tomatoes into a saucepan and break up with a wooden spoon. Add the drained butter beans and black-eyed beans, the garlic purée, tomato purée, sweetcorn and peppers, green beans (not drained), stock, half the herbs and a little salt and pepper. Bring to the boil, reduce the heat, cover and simmer for 5 minutes.**

2. **Empty the dumpling mix into a bowl with the cheese and the rest of the herbs. Add enough cold water to form a soft but not sticky dough. Shape into 8 balls.**

3. Arrange the dumplings around the top of the stew, cover and simmer for 15–20 minutes until fluffy. Serve hot.

Preparation time: 4 minutes
Cooking time: 20–25 minutes

QUICK BEAN BAKE

Serves 2–4

Ingredients	Metric	Imperial	American
Can of ratatouille	425 g	15 oz	1 large
Can of red kidney beans, drained	425 g	15 oz	1 large
Dried mixed herbs	2.5 ml	½ tsp	½ tsp
Pepper			
Breadcrumbs	50 g	2 oz	½ cup
Cheddar cheese, grated	50 g	2 oz	½ cup

I. Heat together the ratatouille, red kidney beans, herbs and pepper in a flameproof casserole dish (Dutch oven).

2. Mix the breadcrumbs and cheese and sprinkle over.

3. Grill (broil) until the cheese has melted and browned.

Preparation time: 3 minutes
Cooking time: 7 minutes

TIP: A slice of bread from a medium sliced loaf is about 25 g/1 oz. Simply crumble between your fingers and thumb to make rough breadcrumbs.

SAUCY PASTA SURPRISE

Serves 4

Ingredients	Metric	Imperial	American
Pasta shapes	225 g	8 oz	8 oz
Can of tomatoes, chopped	400 g	14 oz	1 large
Can of sweetcorn (corn)	200 g	7 oz	1 small
Frozen chopped spinach, thawed	225 g	8 oz	8 oz
Dried oregano	2.5 ml	½ tsp	½ tsp
Salt and pepper			
Packet of cheese sauce mix	1	1	1
Milk or water (according to the packet directions)	300 ml	½ pt	1¼ cups
Cheddar or Parmesan cheese, grated (optional)	50 g	2 oz	½ cup

1. **Cook the pasta according to the packet directions. Drain, stir in the tomatoes, sweetcorn, spinach, oregano and seasoning and heat through until piping hot.**

2. **Make up the cheese sauce according to the packet directions.**

3. **Pile the pasta on warm plates, spoon the sauce over and sprinkle with grated cheese (if using). Serve hot.**

**Preparation time: nil
Cooking time: 15 minutes**

TORTELLINI WITH TOMATO SAUCE

Serves 2

Ingredients	Metric	Imperial	American
Can of tomatoes	400 g	14 oz	1 large
Tomato purée (paste)	15 ml	1 tbsp	1 tbsp
Garlic purée (paste)	2.5 ml	½ tsp	½ tsp
Salt and pepper			
Dried basil	2.5 ml	½ tsp	½ tsp
Dried tortellini stuffed with either spinach and ricotta cheese, 3 cheeses, or mushrooms	250 g	9 oz	9 oz

To serve: Grated cheese (optional) and salad

I. **Put the tomatoes in a pan. Break up well with a wooden spoon.**

2. **Add the tomato purée, garlic purée, a little salt and pepper and the basil.**

3. **Meanwhile, cook the tortellini according to the packet directions. Drain and add to the sauce. Toss well.**

4. **Serve with grated cheese, if liked, and a salad.**

Preparation time: 3 minutes
Cooking time: 12 minutes

CORN FRITTERS WITH PEANUT SAUCE

Serves 3–4

Ingredients	Metric	Imperial	American
For the sauce:			
Can of coconut milk	300 g	11 oz	1 large
Crunchy peanut butter	75 ml	5 tbsp	5 tbsp
Sugar	10 ml	2 tsp	2 tsp
Chilli powder	1.5 ml	¼ tsp	¼ tsp
Vinegar or lemon juice	5 ml	1 tsp	1 tsp
Garlic purée (paste)	2.5 ml	½ tsp	½ tsp
For the fritters:			
Plain (all-purpose) flour	90 ml	6 tbsp	6 tbsp
Eggs	2	2	2
Milk	60 ml	4 tbsp	4 tbsp
Can of sweetcorn (corn), drained	300 g	11 oz	1 large
Salt and pepper			
Oil			

To serve: Vegetable 'dippers'

1. **Put all the ingredients for the sauce in a pan and heat through gently, stirring occasionally, until the sauce boils.**

2. **To make the fritters: put the flour in a bowl. Beat the eggs and milk together. Gradually add to the flour, beating well until smooth.**

3. Add the drained sweetcorn and a little seasoning. Mix well.

4. Heat about 5 mm/¼ in of oil in a large frying pan (skillet), fry (sauté) spoonfuls of the corn batter until golden on the base, turn and fry on the other side. Drain on kitchen paper.

5. Serve the fritters with the hot sauce and sticks of raw vegetables as extra 'dippers'.

Preparation time: 5 minutes
Cooking time: 10 minutes

MIDDLE EASTERN DIP

**Use other pulses such as canned flageolet
or cannellini beans if you prefer.**

Serves 1

Ingredients	Metric	Imperial	American
Can of butter beans, drained	213 g	7½ oz	1 small
Garlic purée (paste)	2.5 ml	½ tsp	½ tsp
Oil	60 ml	4 tbsp	4 tbsp
Vinegar or lemon juice	5 ml	1 tsp	1 tsp
Salt and pepper			
To garnish: Dried mint (optional)			
To serve: Pitta bread and vegetable sticks			

I. **Mash the butter beans and garlic purée in a bowl with a
fork.**

2. **Gradually beat in the oil a spoonful at a time.**

3. **Add the vinegar or lemon juice and season with salt and
pepper.**

4. **Sprinkle with dried mint if using. Serve with pitta bread
and vegetable sticks.**

**Preparation time: 4 minutes
Cooking time: nil**

**TIP: Bought tubs of hummus or taramasalata make a good
quick meal with lots of vegetable dippers and pitta bread,
too.**

TORTILLA
This can be made with leftover cooked potato.
Tortilla is delicious served cold with salad.

Serves 2

Ingredients	Metric	Imperial	American
Large potato, cut into small dice	1	1	1
Small onion, chopped	1	1	1
Oil	15 ml	1 tbsp	1 tbsp
Chopped parsley (optional)	15 ml	1 tbsp	1 tbsp
Salt and pepper			
Eggs, beaten	4	4	4

I. **Put the potato and onion with the oil in a frying pan (skillet) and fry (sauté) for 4 minutes, stirring, until the potato is almost cooked.**

2. **Add the parsley, if using, a little seasoning and the eggs. Cook gently, lifting and stirring at first, until the egg has almost set. Place under a hot grill (broiler) to brown and set the top.**

3. **Serve cut into wedges.**

Preparation time: 5 minutes
Cooking time: 10 minutes

PIPERADE

Serves 2

Ingredients	Metric	Imperial	American
Oil	15 ml	1 tbsp	1 tbsp
Knob of margarine			
Onion, sliced	1	1	1
Green (bell) pepper, sliced	1	1	1
Large tomatoes, quartered	4	4	4
Garlic purée (paste)	2.5 ml	½ tsp	½ tsp
Eggs, beaten	4	4	4
Salt and pepper			
To serve: Crusty bread			

1. **Heat the oil and margarine in a large frying pan (skillet).**

2. **Add the prepared vegetables and garlic purée and fry (sauté) gently for 5 minutes, stirring until soft.**

3. **Add the eggs, season and cook, lifting and stirring gently until set.**

4. **Serve straight from the pan with crusty bread.**

Preparation time: 5–10 minutes
Cooking time: 10 minutes

NO-NONSENSE RATATOUILLE.

Serves 4 (or 2 hot and 2 cold)

Ingredients	Metric	Imperial	American
Small aubergine (eggplant), sliced	1	1	1
Courgettes (zucchini), sliced	3	3	3
Onion, sliced	1	1	1
Green (bell) pepper, sliced	1	1	1
Oil	45 ml	3 tbsp	3 tbsp
Can of tomatoes	400 g	14 oz	1 large
Dried oregano	2.5 ml	½ tsp	½ tsp
Salt and pepper			

To serve: Pasta OR bread and grated parmesan or Cheddar cheese

1. **Put the prepared vegetables in a large pan with the oil and stir over a high heat to coat.**

2. **Add the canned tomatoes and break up with a wooden spoon. Add the oregano and season with salt and pepper. Cover and simmer for 15 minutes, stirring occasionally, until the vegetables are just tender.**

3. **Serve with cooked pasta or bread and grated Parmesan or Cheddar cheese.**

Preparation time: 10 minutes
Cooking time: 20 minutes

TIP: Ratatouille is great cold, too.

QUICK PAN PIZZA

Serves 1–2

Ingredients	Metric	Imperial	American
For the base:			
Self-raising (self-rising) flour	100g	4 oz	1 cup
Pinch of salt			
Oil	45 ml	3 tbsp	3 tbsp
Water to mix			
For the topping:			
Can of tomatoes, drained	227 g	8 oz	1 small
Dried oregano	1.5 ml	¼ tsp	¼ tsp
Cheddar cheese, grated	50 g	2 oz	½ cup
Additional toppings:			

Chopped ham, sliced mushrooms, drained sweetcorn (corn), diced green or red (bell) peppers, pepperami, drained pineapple pieces.

1. Mix the flour with the salt in a bowl. Add 30 ml/2 tbsp of the oil a tablespoon at a time to form a soft but not sticky dough.

2. Squeeze gently into a ball, then flatten out to a round to fit the base of a frying pan (skillet).

3. Heat the remaining oil in the frying pan, add the base and fry (sauté) for about 3 minutes until golden underneath. Turn over.

4. Chop the tomatoes, then spread over the base. Sprinkle with the oregano, add the additonal topping(s) of your choice and top with cheese.

5. Fry for 2–3 minutes, then place the pan under a hot grill (broiler) and cook until the cheese is melted and bubbling. Serve hot.

 Preparation time: 5 minutes
Cooking time: 7 minutes

CURRIED BEAN, RICE AND CHEESE SALAD

Serves 4.

Ingredients	Metric	Imperial	American
Long-grain rice	225 g	8 oz	1 cup
Can of baked beans	400 g	14 oz	1 large
Curry powder	10 ml	2 tsp	2 tsp
Salad cream	15 ml	1 tbsp	1 tbsp
Sultanas (golden raisins)	30 ml	2 tbsp	2 tbsp
Cheddar, Edam or any cheese, cubed	100 g	4 oz	1 cup

To serve: Lettuce leaves

1. Cook the rice in plenty of boiling salted water for 10 minutes or until tender. Drain, rinse and drain again.

2. Place in a bowl. Add the beans, curry powder, salad cream, sultanas and cheese. Toss well.

3. Serve piled on a bed of lettuce.

 Preparation time: 3 minutes
Cooking time: 10–15 minutes

SUMMER TV DINNER

Serves 2

Ingredients	Metric	Imperial	American
Pasta shapes	100 g	4 oz	4 oz
Tomatoes, chopped	2	2	2
Cucumber, diced	5 cm	2 in	2 in
Cheddar cheese, cubed	75 g	3 oz	¾ cup
Can of sweetcorn (corn), drained	200 g	7 oz	1 small
Oil	30 ml	2 tbsp	2 tbsp
Vinegar	10 ml	2 tsp	2 tsp
Pinch of sugar			
Salt and pepper			

1. **Cook the pasta according to the packet directions. Drain, rinse with cold water and drain again.**

2. **Put in a bowl and add the tomatoes, cucumber, cheese and sweetcorn. Mix gently.**

3. **Whisk the remaining ingredients together and pour over. Toss lightly.**

4. **Serve in bowls.**

Preparation time: 5 minutes
Cooking time: 10 minutes

SPAGHETTI WITH BASIL AND MUSHROOMS

Serves 4

Ingredients	Metric	Imperial	American
Spaghetti	350 g	12 oz	12 oz
Margarine	50 g	2 oz	¼ cup
Oil	30 ml	2 tbsp	2 tbsp
Mushrooms, sliced	100 g	4 oz	4 oz
Garlic purée (paste)	5 ml	1 tsp	1 tsp
Pine nuts	50 g	2 oz	½ cup
Parmesan or Cheddar cheese, grated	30 ml	2 tbsp	2 tbsp
Handful of fresh basil leaves, torn into pieces			
Salt and pepper			
To serve: Tomato and onion salad			

1. Cook the spaghetti according to packet directions. Drain in a colander.

2. Melt the margarine and oil in the spaghetti pan and fry (sauté) the mushrooms gently for 3 minutes.

3. Return the spaghetti to the pan with the mushrooms and add the garlic purée, pine nuts, cheese and basil. Toss until piping hot, then season to taste.

4. Serve hot with a tomato and onion salad.

Preparation time: 10 minutes
Cooking time: 12–15 minutes

POULTRY

FEED ME

Chicken and turkey are more economical than most other meats. Look out at your fresh meat counter for turkey steaks (often on special offer), or buy packs of six frozen fillets which are excellent value. Chicken thighs are much cheaper than drumsticks or portions and taste just as good. Stir-fry strips, diced and minced poultry are also good buys. Always make sure frozen chicken is thoroughly defrosted before cooking.

TIP: A small frozen chicken will easily serve four. To divide it into portions, before or after cooking, cut the bird in half straight through the breastbone lengthways, cutting right through the back bone. Then divide each half into quarters behind the leg and thigh so you have two breast and wing portions and two leg and thigh portions.

EXTRA FILLING CHICKEN AND CORN CHOWDER

Serves 4

Ingredients	Metric	Imperial	American
Can of condensed cream of chicken soup	295 g	10½ oz	1 large
Milk	300 ml	½ pt	1¼ cups
Can of sweetcorn (corn)	200 g	7 oz	1 small
Can of new potatoes, drained and diced	300 g	11 oz	1 large
Pinch of chilli powder			
To serve: Crusty bread			

1. **Empty the soup into a saucepan. Fill the empty soup can with milk and gradually blend it in.**

2. **Add the contents of the can of sweetcorn and the diced potatoes and season with the chilli powder.**

3. **Heat through gently, stirring occasionally.**

4. **Serve in soup bowls with crusty bread.**

Preparation time: 1 minute
Cooking time: 3 minutes

LEMON CHICKEN WITH HERBS

Serves 2

Ingredients	Metric	Imperial	American
Chicken portions	2	2	2
Oil	30 ml	2 tbsp	2 tbsp
Salt and pepper			
Dried mixed herbs	5 ml	1 tsp	1 tsp
Lemon juice	45 ml	3 tbsp	3 tbsp

To serve: Sautéed potatoes and courgettes (zucchini) (see page 14)

1. Rub the chicken with a little of the oil, then season with salt and pepper.

2. Grill (broil) the chicken for about 7–8 minutes each side until the skin is crispy and the flesh is almost cooked through.

3. Whisk together the remaining oil, the herbs and lemon juice. Brush over the chicken and continue to grill for another 3–4 minutes until thoroughly cooked. Brush again after 2 minutes.

4. Serve with sautéed potatoes and courgettes.

Preparation time: 3 minutes
Cooking time: about 20 minutes

CRUNCHY TURKEY STEAKS

This dish is equally good made with small boneless pork steaks. Use sage and onion stuffing instead of parsley and thyme.

Serves 2

Ingredients	Metric	Imperial	American
Small turkey steaks	2	2	2
Egg, beaten	1	1	1
Packet of parsley and thyme stuffing (85 g/3½ oz)	½	½	½
Oil			

To serve: Mashed potatoes (see page 13–14) and green beans

1. Put a turkey steak in a plastic bag. Beat with a rolling pin to flatten. Repeat with the other piece.

2. Dip the turkey in beaten egg, then in stuffing mix to coat completely. Shallow fry (sauté) in hot oil for about 3 minutes on each side until golden and cooked through.

3. Serve with mashed potatoes and green beans.

Preparation time: 5 minutes
Cooking time: 6 minutes

SPICY CHICKEN WINGS

**Leave these marinating in the fridge all day
if it's more convenient.**

Serves 2

Ingredients	Metric	Imperial	American
Chicken wings	225 g	8 oz	8 oz
Small onion, finely chopped	1	1	1
Light brown sugar	10 ml	2 tsp	2 tsp
Worcestershire sauce	15 ml	1 tbsp	1 tbsp
Oil	10 ml	2 tsp	2 tsp
Cayenne or chilli powder	2.5 ml	½ tsp	½ tsp
Salt	5 ml	1 tsp	1 tsp
Pepper			

To serve: Crispy potato skins (see page 13) and salad

1. **Place the chicken wings in a bowl. Mix together the remaining ingredients and pour over the chicken wings, rubbing the mixture into the skin. Leave to marinate for at least 2 hours.**

2. **Lift from the marinade and grill (broil) for about 15–20 minutes, turning once or twice, until cooked through and crispy.**

3. **Serve with crispy potato skins and salad.**

**Preparation time: 6 minutes, plus marinating
Cooking time: 15–20 minutes**

MAYBE CHICKEN CHOW MEIN

Serves 2

Ingredients	Metric	Imperial	American
Quick-cook Chinese egg noodles	100 g	4 oz	4 oz
Oil	15 ml	1 tbsp	1 tbsp
Turkey or chicken stir-fry meat	100 g	4 oz	1 cup
Can of stir-fry mixed vegetables, drained	425 g	15 oz	1 large
Garlic purée (paste)	2.5 ml	½ tsp	½ tsp
Soy sauce	15 ml	1 tbsp	1 tbsp
Vinegar	15 ml	1 tbsp	1 tbsp
Ground ginger	5 ml	1 tsp	1 tsp
Light brown sugar	15 ml	1 tbsp	1 tbsp

I. **Cook the noodles according the packet directions.**

2. **Meanwhile, heat the oil in a large pan or wok. Add the remaining ingredients and stir-fry for 5 minutes.**

3. **Stir in the noodles, reheat and serve.**

Preparation time: 10 minutes
Cooking time: 10 minutes

CHICKEN AND COCONUT MASALA

Why not grow a pot of fresh coriander on the kitchen windowsill? Chop a few leaves and throw in at the last moment for a really authentic flavour.

Serves 2

Ingredients	Metric	Imperial	American
Chicken or turkey meat, diced	175 g	6 oz	1½ cups
Small onion, chopped	1	1	1
Small green (bell) pepper sliced (optional)	1	1	1
Mild curry powder	10 ml	2 tsp	2 tsp
Oil	15 ml	1 tbsp	1 tbsp
Chicken stock made with 1 stock cube	200 ml	3 fl oz	1 cup
Packet of creamed coconut	½	½	½
Raisins	15 ml	1 tbsp	1 tbsp
Salt and pepper			

To serve: Plain boiled rice

1. Fry (sauté) the chicken, onion, pepper and curry powder in the oil for 4 minutes, stirring.

2. Add the remaining ingredients. Bring to the boil, then reduce the heat and simmer for about 6 minutes until the chicken is cooked.

3. If the sauce is still a little runny, remove the chicken with a draining spoon and boil the sauce rapidly, stirring, until it has reduced and thickened.

4. Season to taste. Return the chicken to the sauce.

5. Serve on a bed of rice.

Preparation time: 10 minutes
Cooking time: 14–20 minutes

CHEAT CHICKEN MARYLAND

Serves 2

Ingredients	Metric	Imperial	American
Chicken nuggets, crumb-coated	16	16	16
Streaky bacon rashers	2	2	2
Large banana	1	1	1
Oil			

To serve: Potatoes and sweetcorn (corn)

1. Grill (broil) or fry (sauté) the chicken nuggets according to the packet directions. Keep warm.

2. Cut the bacon rashers in half, roll up and grill or fry until cooked through. Keep warm.

3. Cut the banana in half lengthways and then across to make 4 pieces. Fry in a little oil until just softening.

4. Serve with the chicken, bacon, potatoes and sweetcorn.

Preparation time: 5 minutes
Cooking time: 20 minutes

MILD CURRIED CHICKEN

Serves 2

Ingredients	Metric	Imperial	American
Chicken portions	2	2	2
Plain (all-purpose) flour	15 ml	1 tbsp	1 tbsp
Salt and pepper			
Good knob of margarine			
Curry powder or paste	5 ml	1 tsp	1 tsp
Can of condensed cream of mushroom soup	295 g	10½ oz	1 small;

To serve: Oven-cooked rice (see page 15) and a green vegetable (see page 14)

1. **Wipe the chicken with kitchen paper. Mix the flour with a little salt and pepper and use to coat the chicken.**

2. **Melt the margarine in a flameproof casserole (Dutch oven) and fry (sauté) the chicken on all sides to brown.**

3. **Drain off all but 15 ml/1 tbsp of the fat. Stir in the curry powder or paste, then blend in the soup.**

4. **Cook in a preheated oven at 180°C/350°F/gas mark 4 for 1 hour or until the chicken is tender.**

5. **Serve with oven-cooked rice and a green vegetable.**

Preparation time: 5 minutes
Cooking time: about 1 hour

MEDITERRANEAN CHICKEN

This is great with lamb chops, too,
if you can find a bargain.

Serves 2

Ingredients	Metric	Imperial	American
Onion, chopped	1	1	1
Oil	15 ml	1 tbsp	1 tbsp
Chicken portions	2	2	2
Salt and pepper			
Can of condensed tomato soup	295 g	10½ oz	1 small
Dried basil	5 ml	1 tsp	1 tsp
To serve: Jacket or roast potatoes (see pages 13 or 14) and salad			

1. In a flameproof casserole (Dutch oven), fry (sauté) the onion in the oil for 2 minutes. Add the chicken, skin-side down, and fry for 2 minutes to brown.

2. Turn the chicken skin-side up, sprinkle with salt and pepper and spoon the soup over. Add the basil.

3. Cover and cook in a preheated oven at 180°C/350°F/gas mark 4 for 1 hour or until the chicken is tender. Stir occasionally and add a little water if necessary.

4. Serve with jacket or roast potatoes and salad.

Preparation time: 5 minutes
Cooking time: about 1 hour

CHICKEN AND VEGETABLE MORNAY

Serves 2

Ingredients	Metric	Imperial	American
Packet of cheese sauce mix and milk according to the packet directions	1	1	1
OR 1 quantity of cheese sauce (see Basic Macaroni Cheese, page 49)			
Cooked leftover vegetables, chopped (or frozen vegetables, cooked)	225 g	8 oz	2 cups
Cooked chicken, diced	175 g	6 oz	1½ cups
Grated nutmeg (optional)	1.5 ml	¼ tsp	¼ tsp
Packet of plain or cheese and onion crisps (chips)	1	1	1
To serve: Crusty bread			

1. **Make up the cheese sauce.**

2. **Stir in the vegetables, chicken and nutmeg, if using. Heat through for 3 minutes, stirring occasionally.**

3. **Spoon on to warm plates and top with crushed crisps.**

4. **Serve with crusty bread.**

Preparation time: 3 minutes
Cooking time: about 10 minutes

Variation: Substitute a drained can of tuna for the chicken.

GRILLED CHICKEN WITH GARLIC AND HERB SAUCE

This sauce can also be served with fish or vegetables.

Serves 2

Ingredients	Metric	Imperial	American
Chicken portions	2	2	2
OR chicken thighs	4	4	4
Oil			
Cornflour (cornstarch)	10 ml	2 tsp	2 tsp
Milk	150 ml	¼ pt	⅔ cup
Knob of margarine			
Garlic and herb soft cheese	50 g	2 oz	¼ cup
Salt and pepper			

To serve: Savoury vegetable rice

1. Brush the chicken pieces with oil and season lightly. Grill (broil) for about 20 minutes, turning occasionally until crisp, golden and cooked through.

2. Meanwhile, whisk the cornflour with a little of the milk in a saucepan until smooth. Stir in the remaining milk. Add the margarine.

3. Bring to the boil, stirring until thickened. Add the cheese in small pieces and continue stirring over a gentle heat until blended. Season with salt and pepper.

4. Transfer the chicken to warm plates and spoon the sauce over. Serve with savoury vegetable rice.

Preparation time: 2 minutes
Cooking time: 20 minutes

CHINESE-STYLE CHICKEN WITH NUTS AND RAISINS

Serves 2

Ingredients	Metric	Imperial	American
Boneless chicken thighs	2	2	2
Oil	15 ml	1 tbsp	1 tbsp
Small onion, sliced	1	1	1
Carrot, grated	1	1	1
Bean sprouts	100 g	4 oz	1 cup
Peanuts and raisins	50 g	2 oz	½ cup
Chicken stock, made with ½ stock cube	150 ml	¼ pt	⅔ cup
Cornflour (cornstarch)	7.5 ml	½ tbsp	½ tbsp
Soy sauce	10 ml	2 tsp	2 tsp

To serve: Chinese egg noodles sprinkled with soy sauce

1. Cut the chicken into neat strips.

2. Heat the oil in a wok or large frying pan (skillet). Stir-fry (sauté) the chicken, onion and carrot for 5 minutes until cooked through.

3. Add the bean sprouts, peanuts and raisins and stock.

4. Blend the cornflour with the soy sauce and stir into the pan. Bring to the boil and cook for 2 minutes.

5. Serve with egg noodles seasoned with soy sauce.

Preparation time: 10–15 minutes
Cooking time: 10 minutes

SPANISH RICE
Serve this hot one day and cold the next.

Serves 4 (or 2 hot and 2 cold)

Ingredients	Metric	Imperial	American
Chicken or turkey, diced	200 g	7 oz	1¾ cups
Small green (bell) pepper, diced	1	1	1
Oil	30 ml	2 tbsp	2 tbsp
Long-grain rice	225 g	8 oz	1 cup
Chicken or vegetable stock, made with 2 stock cubes	600 ml	1 pt	2½ cups
Frozen peas with sweetcorn (corn)	100 g	4 oz	1 cup
Tomatoes, roughly chopped	2	2	2
Can of tuna, drained	85 g	3½ oz	1 small
Salt and pepper			

1. Fry (sauté) the chicken or turkey and the pepper in the oil for 2 minutes, stirring.

2. Add the rice and stir for 1 minute.

3. Pour on the stock, bring to the boil, cover and simmer for 10 minutes.

4. Add the peas and sweetcorn, tomatoes and tuna, re-cover and cook for a further 10 minutes until the rice is cooked and has absorbed nearly all the liquid. Season to taste.

Preparation time: 10 minutes
Cooking time: 25 minutes

ONE-STEP ROAST CHICKEN

Use as many vegetables as you can eat. I usually allow
4 pieces each of potato, carrot and parsnip and 1–2 small
onions per person.

Serves 4 (or 2 hot and 2 cold)

Ingredients	Metric	Imperial	American
Small roasting chicken, frozen and thawed	1.2 kg	2¾ lb	2¾ lb
Dried mixed herbs	5 ml	1 tsp	1 tsp
Oil			
Salt			
Potatoes, scrubbed	4	4	4
Carrots	4	4	4
Large parsnip	1	1	1
Smallish onions	4–8	4–8	4–8
Plain (all-purpose) flour	15 ml	1 tbsp	1 tbsp
Chicken or vegetable stock cube	1	1	1
Pepper			
To serve: Peas (optional)			

1. Remove the giblets from inside the bird. Wipe inside and
   out with kitchen paper and pull off any excess fat from
   around the body cavity wall. (You can feel it just inside
   the opening if there is any.)

2. Put the herbs in the body cavity, then place the bird in a
   large roasting tin (baking pan). Rub all over with oil and
   a little salt.

3. Cut the scrubbed potatoes into even-sized pieces. Peel
    and cut the carrots and parsnips into chunky fingers.
    Peel the onions, but leave whole. Put all except the
    onions in a pan, cover with water and bring to the boil.
    Cook for 3 minutes, then drain, reserving 300 ml/½ pt/
    1¼ cups of the cooking water. Arrange all the vegetables
    around the chicken and drizzle with oil, then toss to coat
    completely. Sprinkle with a little salt.

4. Roast in a preheated oven at 190°C/375°F/gas mark 5
    for 1½ hours or until the chicken and vegetables are
    golden and cooked through. Turn the vegetables once or
    twice during cooking.

5. Transfer the chicken to a plate and the vegetables to a
    warm dish and keep warm.

6. Mix the flour with a little cold water until smooth then
    blend in the reserved vegetable water. Stir into the juices
    in the roasting tin and crumble in the stock cube. Bring
    to the boil on top of the stove, stirring all the time until
    thickened. Season to taste.

7. Carve or cut the chicken into quarters and serve with the
    roasted vegetables, peas, if liked, and the gravy.

Preparation time: 15 minutes
Cooking time: about 1 hour 45 minutes

NO-FUSS CURRIED CHICKEN MAYONNAISE

This is a great way of using up One-step Roast Chicken (see page 90), but it makes a little chicken go a long way even if you buy it ready-cooked.

Serves 4

Ingredients	Metric	Imperial	American
Packet of savoury rice with mushrooms	1	1	1
Small chicken, cooked	½	½	½
Mayonnaise	45 ml	3 tbsp	3 tbsp
Mango chutney	20 ml	4 tsp	4 tsp
Curry paste	10 ml	2 tsp	2 tsp

To serve: Popadoms

1. Cook the savoury rice according to the packet directions. Drain, spoon into a ring on a large serving plate and leave until cold.

2. Pick all the meat off the chicken and cut into bite-sized pieces.

3. Mix the mayonnaise with the chutney and curry paste. Fold in the chicken and pile into the centre of the cold rice.

4. Serve with the popadoms.

Preparation time: 8 minutes
Cooking time: about 15 minutes, plus cooling

TURKEY STROGANOFF

Serves 2

Ingredients	Metric	Imperial	American
Small onion, sliced	1	1	1
Mushrooms, sliced	50 g	2 oz	2 oz
Knob of margarine			
Turkey stir-fry meat	175 g	6 oz	1½ cups
Wine, beer or cider	15 ml	1 tbsp	1 tbsp
Plain yoghurt	150 ml	¼ pt	⅔ cup
Salt and pepper			
To serve: Tagliatelle and a green salad			

I. **Fry (sauté) the onion and mushrooms for 3 minutes in the margarine.**

2. **Add the turkey and fry for 4–5 minutes until cooked through.**

3. **Stir in the wine, beer or cider and bubble briefly. Stir in the yoghurt and heat through but do not boil. Season to taste.**

4. **Serve with tagliatelle and a green salad.**

Preparation time: 10 minutes
Cooking time: 10–12 minutes

OTHER MEATY MEALS

FEED ME

Most meat is fairly expensive. There is no doubt that mince is not only a good buy but also very versatile. Large packs of free-flow beef, lamb or pork mince are ideal as you can use as little or as much as you need at any time – and you can use it from frozen. For added economy look for mince with soya protein. It's certainly cheap and tastes OK but the texture isn't as good. Some cuts of pork such as belly slices or shoulder steaks won't mean taking out a mortgage, but unfortunately most cuts of beef, lamb or pork – even the tougher cuts like shin of beef – can be quite dear (and they take a long time to cook which you probably don't want). For this reason I have included some really tasty ideas using canned steak, corned beef and even frankfurters. With a little tarting up they can produce excellent results in next to no time. Even canned ham is a useful standby. And you'll be amazed what you can do with some good old bangers or the odd pepperami stick!

TIP: Keep your eyes open for good deals on chops or steaks. If you do treat yourself, the best way to cook them is to brush with a little oil or dot with margarine, season lightly and grill (broil) or fry until browned and cooked to your liking. Then serve with any vegetables of your choice or pasta with tomatoes.

BUMPER BURGERS

Serves 2

Ingredients	Metric	Imperial	American
Minced (ground) beef, lamb, pork or turkey	225 g	8 oz	2 cups
Small onion, chopped	1	1	1
Mustard	2.5 ml	½ tsp	½ tsp
Tomato purée (paste)	2.5 ml	½ tsp	½ tsp
Worcestershire sauce	5 ml	1 tsp	1 tsp
Salt and pepper			
Small egg, beaten	1	1	1

To serve: Burger buns and salad

1. Mix together the meat, onion, mustard, tomato purée and Worcestershire sauce, seasoning to taste with salt and pepper.

2. Bind the mixture with the egg (you might not need to use all of it). Shape into 2 burgers and chill (if time) before cooking.

3. Grill (broil) for about 6 minutes on each side, depending on the thickness, until cooked through.

4. Serve in burger buns with salad.

Preparation time: 5 minutes
Cooking time: 12 minutes

CHUCK-IT-TOGETHER MEAT LOAF

Serves 4 (or 2 hot and 2 cold)

Ingredients	Metric	Imperial	American
Minced (ground) beef, lamb, pork or turkey	450 g	1 lb	4 cups
Onion, finely chopped	1	1	1
Dried mixed herbs or basil	5 ml	1 tsp	1 tsp
Grated rind and juice of ½ lemon			
Worcestershire sauce	10 ml	2 tsp	2 tsp
Red wine	45 ml	3 tbsp	3 tbsp
Tomato purée (paste)	10 ml	2 tbsp	2 tbsp
Salt and pepper			
Small egg, beaten	1	1	1

To serve: Canned tomatoes, crusty bread or salad and pickles

1. **Mix together all the ingredients and press into a greased 450 g/1 lb loaf tin (pan) or deep ovenproof dish. Cover with foil and bake at 180°C/350°F/gas mark 4 for 1 hour.**

2. **Cool slightly, then turn out.**

3. **Serve hot sliced with canned tomatoes and crusty bread, or cold with salad and pickles.**

Preparation time: 5 minutes
Cooking time: 1 hour

HASTY PASTA

Serves 2

Ingredients	Metric	Imperial	American
Pasta shapes	100 g	4 oz	4 oz
Can of minced (ground) steak with onions	177 g	6 oz	1 small
Dried mixed herbs	2.5 ml	½ tsp	½ tsp
Cheddar cheese, grated	50 g	2 oz	½ cup
Tomatoes, sliced (optional)	1–2	1–2	1–2

To serve: Salad

I. **Cook the pasta according to the packet directions. Drain.**

2. **Return to the saucepan, add the mince and season with the herbs.**

3. **Heat through, stirring gently, until piping hot.**

4. **Turn on to warm plates and sprinkle cheese over.**

5. **Arrange the tomato slices around, if using, and serve with salad.**

Preparation time: 2 minutes
Cooking time: about 15 minutes

EVERYDAY SPAGHETTI BOLOGNESE

It's worth making enough for 4 people as the sauce keeps
well in the fridge for several days. As a guide for quantities
of spaghetti, cook 50–100 g/2–4 oz per person.
You can always have lots of pasta and less sauce if more
people turn up!

Serves 4

Ingredients	Metric	Imperial	American
Minced (ground) beef or lamb	350 g	12 oz	3 cups
Onion, chopped	1	1	1
Garlic purée (paste)	2.5 ml	½ tsp	½ tsp
Can of tomatoes, chopped	400 g	14 oz	1 large
Tomato purée (paste)	15 ml	1 tbsp	1 tbsp
Salt and pepper			
Dried oregano	5 ml	1 tsp	1 tsp
Pinch of caster (superfine)			
Spaghetti	350 g	12 oz	12 oz
Parmesan cheese, grated			

1. Put the meat, onion and garlic purée in a saucepan.
   Cook, stirring, until the grains of meat are brown and
   separate.

2. Add the remaining ingredients except the spaghetti and
   Parmesan cheese. Stir well. Bring to the boil, reduce the
   heat, half-cover and simmer gently for 15–20 minutes
   until a rich sauce has formed. Stir gently occasionally.

3. Meanwhile, cook the spaghetti according to the packet
   directions. Drain and pile on to serving plates. Spoon
   the sauce over and top with Parmesan cheese.

Preparation time: 5 minutes
Cooking time: 20 minutes

TIP: To make a lasagne, layer the sauce with no-need-to-pre-cook lasagne, top with cheese sauce (see page **49**) and bake at 190°C/375°F/gas mark 5 for 35 minutes.

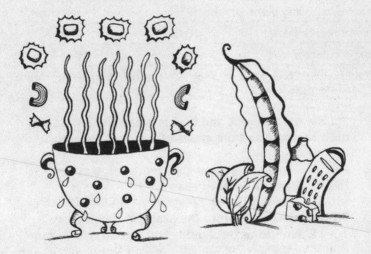

QUICK CHILLI

Serves 2–3

Ingredients	Metric	Imperial	American
Onion, chopped	1	1	1
Garlic purée (paste)	2.5 ml	½ tsp	½ tsp
Minced (ground) beef	175 g	6 oz	1½ cups
Hot chilli powder	2.5 ml	½ tsp	½ tsp
Ground cumin (optional)	2.5 ml	½ tsp	½ tsp
Dried oregano or mixed herbs	2.5 ml	½ tsp	½ tsp
Can of tomatoes	400 g	14 oz	1 large
Can of red kidney beans, drained	425 g	15 oz	1 large
Tomato purée (paste)	10 ml	2 tsp	2 tsp
Salt and pepper			

To serve: Plain boiled rice or crispy taco shells, grated cheddar cheese and shredded lettuce

1. Put the onion, garlic and beef in a pan and fry (sauté) until browned and the grains of meat are separate.

2. Add the remaining ingredients and break up the tomatoes with a wooden spoon.

3. Bring to the boil, reduce the heat and simmer for 10–15 minutes or until pulpy and a good rich colour.

4. Serve with plain boiled rice, or in crispy taco shells with grated cheese and shredded lettuce to sprinkle over.

Preparation time: 5 minutes
Cooking time: 15–20 minutes

PASTA PLEASE

Serves 2

Ingredients	Metric	Imperial	American
Pasta shapes	100 g	4 oz	4 oz
Small onion, chopped	1	1	1
Garlic purée (paste)	2.5 ml	½ tsp	½ tsp
Minced (ground) beef	100 g	4 oz	1 cup
Can of tomatoes	400 g	14 oz	1 large
Dried mixed herbs	2.5 ml	½ tsp	½ tsp
Salt and pepper			
Cheddar cheese, grated	50 g	2 oz	½ cup

To serve: Mixed salad

1. Cook the pasta according to the packet directions, then drain.

2. Use the same pan to fry (sauté) the onion, garlic purée and beef, stirring until browned and the meat grains are separate.

3. Add the tomatoes, break up with a wooden spoon. Stir in the herbs and a little salt and pepper. Bring to the boil, reduce the heat and simmer for 10 minutes until cooked through and the sauce is pulpy.

4. Stir in the pasta. Spoon on to plates and sprinkle with cheese.

5. Serve hot with a mixed salad.

Preparation time: 5 minutes
Cooking time: 15 minutes

BEEF IN BEER

Serves 2

Ingredients	Metric	Imperial	American
Can of stewed steak in gravy	440 g	15½ oz	1 large
Beer	30 ml	2 tbsp	2 tbsp
Instant mashed potato powder	15 ml	1 tbsp	1 tbsp
Slices French bread	4–6	4–6	4–6
Margarine	15 g	½ oz	1 tbsp
Mustard	5 ml	1 tsp	1 tsp

To serve: Boiled potatoes in their skins (see page 12) and green beans

1. Empty the meat into a small flameproof casserole (Dutch oven) with the beer. Stir well. Heat until bubbling.

2. Sprinkle the instant mashed potato over and stir in to thicken.

3. Meanwhile, toast the slices of French bread on one side. Mash the margarine and mustard together and spread on the untoasted sides.

4. Arrange around the top of the meat. Place under a hot grill (broiler) until toasted and bubbling.

5. Serve hot with boiled potatoes and green beans.

Preparation time: 5 minutes
Cooking time: 10 minutes

TIP: To make this go round for 3 or 4 people, add a layer of a 400 g/14 oz/1 large can of red cabbage with apple once you've thickened the gravy. Cover and heat through for 2 minutes before topping with the mustard toast.

BEEF AND VEG IN WINE

Serves 2–3

Ingredients	Metric	Imperial	American
Small onion, finely chopped	1	1	1
Oil	15 ml	1 tbsp	1 tbsp
Can of stewed steak	440 g	15½ oz	1 large
Red wine	150 ml	¼ pt	⅔ cup
Can of button mushrooms	300 g	11 oz	1 small
Can of sliced carrots	275 g	10 oz	1 small
Dried mixed herbs	2.5 ml	½ tsp	½ tsp
Pinch of caster (superfine) sugar			
Cornflour (cornstarch)	20 ml	4 tsp	4 tsp
Salt and pepper			

To serve: Mashed potatoes (see page 13–14)

1. **Fry (sauté) the onion in the oil for 3 minutes until soft but not brown.**

2. **Add the steak and wine and heat through, stirring.**

3. **Drain the mushrooms and carrots, reserving 30 ml/ 2 tbsp of the mushroom liquid. Add the vegetables, herbs and sugar to the pan and heat gently until bubbling.**

4. **Blend the cornflour with the reserved mushroom liquid. Stir gently into the pan and cook until thickened. Taste and season if necessary.**

5. **Serve with mashed potatoes.**

Preparation time: 5 minutes
Cooking time: 10 minutes

INTERNATIONAL BEEF POT

Serves 2–3

Ingredients	Metric	Imperial	American
Can of stewed steak with or without gravy	440 g	15½ oz	1 large
Can of water chestnuts	225 g	8 oz	1 small
Can of condensed mushroom soup	295 g	10½ oz	1 small
Large potatoes, thinly sliced	2	2	2

To serve: Green vegetable [see page 14]

1. **Empty the meat into a shallow ovenproof dish and break up with a wooden spoon.**

2. **Drain and slice the water chestnuts and scatter over.**

3. **Spoon over half the can of soup.**

4. **Arrange the sliced potatoes neatly in a single layer over the top.**

5. **Thin the remaining soup slightly with water and spoon over.**

6. **Bake in a hot oven at 200°C/400°F/gas mark 6 for about 45 minutes until the potatoes are cooked and the top is a golden brown.**

7. **Serve with a green vegetable.**

Preparation time: 5 minutes
Cooking time: 45 minutes

TOWN HOUSE PIE

Serves 2

Ingredients	Metric	Imperial	American
Can of minced (ground) steak with onion	177 g	6 oz	1 small
Can of baked beans	225 g	8 oz	1 small
Worcestershire sauce	5 ml	1 tsp	1 tsp
Pinch of dried thyme or mixed herbs			
2 servings of instant mashed potato			
Cheddar cheese, grated	50 g	2 oz	½ cup

To serve: Crusty bread and a green vegetable (see page 14)

1. **Put the meat, beans, Worcestershire sauce and herbs in a small flameproof casserole and heat through until piping hot, stirring occasionally.**

2. **Meanwhile, make up the potato according to the packet directions. Pile on top of the meat mixture and sprinkle with cheese.**

3. **Place under a hot grill (broiler) until golden and bubbling.**

4. **Serve with crusty bread and a green vegetable.**

Preparation time: 5 minutes
Cooking time: about 5 minutes

CHUCK-IT-TOGETHER MOUSSAKA

The cinnamon gives an authentic Greek flavour and is useful
for flavouring lots of things from apples to chocolate.

Serves 3–4

Ingredients	Metric	Imperial	American
Potatoes, scrubbed and sliced (not peeled)	450 g	1 lb	1 lb
OR can of potatoes	500 g	1 lb	2 oz
Can of minced (ground) steak with onion	425 g	15 oz	1 large
Garlic purée	2.5 ml	½ tsp	½ tsp
Tomato purée (paste)	15 ml	1 tbsp	1 tbsp
Cinnamon (optional)	5 ml	1 tsp	1 tsp
Plain yoghurt	150 ml	¼ pt	⅔ cup
Egg	1	1	1
Salt and pepper			
Cheddar cheese, grated	50 g	2 oz	½ cup

To serve: Salad

1. Boil the potatoes in salted water for about 5 minutes
   until tender, then drain. If using canned potatoes, drain
   and slice them.

2. Mix the mince with the garlic purée, tomato purée and
   cinnamon, if using. Layer the potatoes and meat mixture
   in an ovenproof dish, finishing with a layer of potatoes.

3. Beat the yoghurt with the egg and a little salt and
   pepper. Stir in the cheese. Pour over the potatoes.

4. Bake in a preheated oven at 190°C/375°F/gas mark 5 for about 35 minutes until bubbling, golden and the top has set.

5. Serve with a salad.

 Preparation time: 5 minutes
Cooking time: 35 minutes

QUICK CASSOULET

Serves 4

Ingredients	Metric	Imperial	American
Cooked ham slices, diced	2	2	2
Can of frankfurters, drained and cut into pieces	400 g	14 oz	1 large
Can of red kidney beans, drained	425 g	15 oz	1 large
Can of baked beans	400 g	14 oz	1 large
Can of cut green beans, drained	278 g	10 oz	1 small

To serve: Crusty bread

1. Put all the ingredients in a large pan. Heat through, stirring gently, for about 5 minutes or until piping hot.

2. Serve in soup bowls with crusty bread.

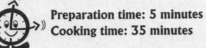 Preparation time: 2 minutes
Cooking time: 7 minutes

MEXICAN MEAL IN MINUTES

For less fire, use half the amount of chilli powder.

Serves 2

Ingredients	Metric	Imperial	American
Can of minced (ground) steak with onions	117 g	6 oz	1 small
Tomato purée (paste)	10 ml	2 tsp	2 tsp
Chilli powder	2.5 ml	½ tsp	½ tsp
Garlic purée (paste)	1.5 ml	¼ tsp	¼ tsp
Can of red kidney beans, drained	425 g	15 oz	1 large
Taco shells	6	6	6

To serve: Shredded lettuce, chopped tomato and cheddar cheese, grated

1. **Put the mince in a pan with the tomato purée, chilli powder, garlic purée and beans. Heat through, stirring until bubbling.**

2. **Warm the taco shells (if liked) according to the packet directions. Spoon the chilli mixture into the shells.**

3. **Serve with shredded lettuce, chopped tomato and cheese to spoon on top of the chilli.**

Preparation time: 5 minutes
Cooking time: 5 minutes

PAN HASH

Serves 4 (or 2 hot and 2 cold)

Ingredients	Metric	Imperial	American
Onion, chopped	1	1	1
Oil	15 ml	1 tbsp	1 tbsp
Cooked potatoes, diced	450 g	1 lb	1 lb
Can of corned beef, diced	350 g	12 oz	1 large
Can of baked beans in tomato sauce	400 g	14 oz	1 large
Brown table sauce	15 ml	1 tbsp	1 tbsp
Salt and pepper			

To serve: Crusty bread and salad

I. **Fry (sauté) the onion in the oil for 3 minutes until soft but not brown.**

2. **Mix in the remaining ingredients and fry for 5 minutes, turning the mixture occasionally.**

3. **Press down with a fish slice and continue frying for a further 5 minutes without disturbing until crisp and brown underneath.**

4. **Serve straight from the pan with crusty bread and salad.**

Preparation time: 5 minutes
Cooking time: 13 minutes

TIP: Serve any remaining hash cold in split pitta bread with some shredded salad for a filling lunch or supper.

SAUCY BROCCOLI AND HAM

Serves 2

Ingredients	Metric	Imperial	American
Broccoli	225 g	8 oz	8 oz
Ham slices	2	2	2
Plain (all-purpose) flour	30 ml	2 tbsp	2 tbsp
Knob of margarine			
Milk	150 ml	¼ pt	⅔ cup
Cheddar cheese, grated	50 g	2 oz	½ cup
Salt and pepper			
To serve: Crusty bread			

1. Separate the broccoli into florets and cook in boiling salted water for about 5 minutes until tender.

2. Lay side by side in a buttered ovenproof dish. Top with the ham.

3. Whisk the flour and margarine into the milk in a pan. Bring to the boil and boil for 2 minutes, whisking all the time until thickened and smooth. Stir in most of the cheese and season to taste.

4. Pour the sauce over the broccoli and ham. Sprinkle with the remaining cheese and grill (broil) for about 3 minutes until golden brown. Serve with crusty bread.

Preparation time: 10 minutes
Cooking time: 10 minutes

ITALIAN-STYLE HAM AND PEAS

Serves 2

Ingredients	Metric	Imperial	American
Onion, finely chopped	1	1	1
Margarine	50 g	2 oz	¼ cup
Oil	15 ml	1 tbsp	1 tbsp
Cooked ham pieces	50 g	2 oz	½ cup
Frozen peas	50 g	2 oz	½ cup
Penne or other pasta	100 g	4 oz	4 oz
Parmesan cheese, grated	30 ml	2 tbsp	2 tbsp
Salt and pepper			

1. **Fry (sauté) the onion gently in the margarine and oil until soft but not brown.**

2. **Meanwhile, cut the ham into very small cubes, discarding any fat or gristle.**

3. **Add the ham and peas to the onions. Cover, reduce the heat and cook gently for 5 minutes, stirring occasionally.**

4. **Cook the pasta according to the packet directions. Drain and return to the saucepan. Add the sauce, cheese and salt and pepper to taste. Toss well.**

5. **Pile on to warm plates and serve.**

Preparation time: 5 minutes
Cooking time: 15 minutes

STICKY BANGERS WITH RICE

Serves 2

Ingredients	Metric	Imperial	American
Long-grain rice	100 g	4 oz	½ cup
Can of red kidney beans, drained	425 g	15 oz	1 large
Salt and pepper			
Chipolata sausages	8	8	8
Knob of margarine			
Vinegar	15 ml	1 tbsp	1 tbsp
Tomato purée (paste)	15 ml	1 tbsp	1 tbsp
Brown table sauce	10 ml	2 tsp	2 tsp
Golden (light corn) syrup	15 ml	1 tbsp	1 tbsp

1. Cook the rice in plenty of boiling salted water for 10 minutes or until tender. Drain and return to the pan.

2. Stir in the beans and a little salt and pepper. Cover and heat very gently, stirring until hot.

3. Meanwhile, fry (sauté) the sausages in a large frying pan (skillet) with no extra fat for about 10 minutes until cooked through and browned. Remove from the pan.

4. Drain off the fat, then stir in the margarine until melted and blend in the remaining ingredients. Return the sausages to the pan and spoon the glaze over them. Cook for about 3 minutes until stickily coated.

5. Pile the rice mixture on to serving plates and top with the sausages. Serve hot.

Preparation time: 5 minutes
Cooking time: 13 minutes

DELUXE GRILL

Packs of 2 pre-formed round ham steaks are on the shelves with the packs of bacon. They're much cheaper than their royal cousins, gammon steaks, and are very tasty.

Serves 2

Ingredients	Metric	Imperial	American
Round ham steaks	2	2	2
Can of pineapple chunks	200 g	7 oz	1 small
Tomatoes, chopped	2	2	2
Processed cheese slices	2	2	2

To serve: Crusty bread or potatoes and green beans

1. Snip the edges of the ham steaks with scissors to prevent curling.

2. Drain and roughly chop the pineapple and mix with the tomatoes.

3. Grill (broil) the ham for 3 minutes on each side.

4. Spread the pineapple mixture over the ham, and top with a slice of cheese.

5. Return to the grill (broiler) until the cheese has melted and the fruit is hot.

6. Serve with crusty bread or potatoes and green beans.

Preparation time: 10 minutes
Cooking time: 15 minutes

TIP: Use a small can of ham instead of steaks. Remove from the can and cut into 3 or 4 thick slices, discarding any jelly. Grill (broil) for 1 minute on each side, then add the pineapple mixture and continue as above. Serve 2 slices per person.

AUSTRIAN PORK CHOPS

Serves 2

Ingredients	Metric	Imperial	American
Pork shoulder steaks	2	2	2
Oil	15 ml	1 tbsp	1 tbsp
Small onion, thinly sliced	1	1	1
Garlic purée (paste)	1.5 ml	¼ tsp	¼ tsp
Small cabbage, shredded	¼	¼	¼
Vegetable stock, made with ½ stock cube	150 ml	¼ pt	⅔ cup
Caraway seeds	15 ml	1 tbsp	1 tbsp
Salt and pepper			
Potatoes, thinly sliced	2	2	2
Knob of margarine			

1. Fry (sauté) the pork steaks in the oil in a deep frying pan (skillet) for 2 minutes on each side to brown. Remove from the pan.

2. Add the onion, garlic purée and cabbage and fry for 2 minutes. Add the stock.

3. Lay the pork steaks on top, sprinkle with the caraway seeds and a little salt and pepper. Cover with the sliced potatoes and dot with margarine. Cover the pan with foil or a lid, reduce the heat and simmer for 20 minutes until tender. Serve straight from the pan.

Preparation time: 10 minutes
Cooking time: 25 minutes

CLEVER HAM CASSEROLE

This is great when you've got to cook for several people. Or have some hot and eat the rest cold for the next couple of days

Serves 4–6 (or 2 hot plus cold leftovers)

Ingredients	Metric	Imperial	American
Long-grain rice	350 g	12 oz	1½ cups
Chicken or vegetable stock, made with 2 stock cubes	750 ml	1 1/2 pts	3 cups
Can of ham, diced	450 g	1 lb	1 large
Eggs, beaten	2	2	2
Can of condensed celery soup	298 g	10½ oz	1 small
Milk	120 ml	4 fl oz	½ cup
Frozen peas	50 g	2 oz	½ cup
Dried mixed herbs	2.5 ml	½ tsp	½ tsp
Tomato wedges			

1. Place the rice in a pan. Add the stock and bring to the boil, stirring. Cover, reduce the heat and cook gently for 15 minutes or until the rice is tender and has absorbed the liquid.

2. Add the ham, including any jelly, and the remaining ingredients, except the tomato wedges.

3. Toss over a gentle heat until creamy and piping hot. Garnish with the tomato wedges and serve hot.

Preparation time: 5 minutes
Cooking time: 18 minutes

SWEET AND SOUR PORK SLICES

Serves 2

Ingredients	Metric	Imperial	American
Belly pork slices	4	4	4
Cornflour (cornstarch)	10 ml	2 tsp	2 tsp
Vinegar	15 ml	1 tbsp	1 tbsp
Can of crushed pineapple	250 g	9 oz	1 small
Tomato ketchup (catsup)	30 ml	2 tbsp	2 tbsp
Soy sauce	15 ml	1 tbsp	1 tbsp
Cucumber, diced	¼	¼	¼
Large carrot, grated	1	1	1

To serve: Plain boiled rice

I. Discard any rind or bones from the pork and cut into chunks. Fry (sauté) over a moderate heat for about 10 minutes, turning occasionally, until browned and cooked through. Remove from the pan.

2. Blend the cornflour with the vinegar.

3. Add the remaining ingredients to the pan and blend in the cornflour mixture. Bring to the boil, stirring. Return the pork to the pan and simmer for 3 minutes, stirring occasionally.

4. Serve with boiled rice.

 Preparation time: 5 minutes
Cooking time: 20–25 minutes

CHEESE AND SAUSAGE BURGERS

Sausagemeat usually comes in 450 g/1 lb packs so it's worth making up all 4 burgers and freezing the remainder to cook on other days. Alternatively make only 2 burgers and use the rest for Toad-In-The-Hole (see page 118).

Serves 4

Ingredients	Metric	Imperial	American
Pork sausagemeat	450 g	1 lb	4 cups
Baby Bel cheeses, rind removed	4	4	4
OR Cheddar or Edam cheese cut into 2.5 cm/1 in cubes			
Oil	15 ml	1 tbsp	1 tbsp
Tomato relish	30 ml	2 tbsp	2 tbsp
Burger buns	4	4	4

To serve: Salad

1. Shape the sausagement into 8 small flat cakes.

2. Place a Baby Bel or cube of other cheese in the centre of each of 4 cakes, then top with the remainder, pressing the edges well together to seal.

3. Brush with oil, then grill (broil) or fry (sauté) in the oil for 4–5 minutes on each side, turning once, until crisp, golden and cooked through. Drain on kitchen paper.

4. Spread with a little tomato relish and serve in the buns with salad.

Preparation time: 5 minutes
Cooking time: 8–10 minutes

TOAD-IN-THE-HOLE

Serves 2

Ingredients	Metric	Imperial	American
Chipolata sausages or sausagemeat	225 g	8 oz	2 cups
Oil	30 ml	2 tbsp	2 tbsp
Plain (all-purpose) flour	50 g	2 oz	½ cup
Pinch of salt			
Egg	1	1	1
Milk and water, mixed	150 ml	¼ pt	⅔ cup
Dried mixed herbs (optional)	2.5 ml	½ tsp	½ tsp

To serve: Baked beans or canned tomatoes and a leafy green vegetable (see page 14)

1. Put the sausages in a shallow baking tin (pan) or roll the sausagement into balls and put in the pan. Add the oil, then cook in a preheated oven at 200°C/400°F/gas mark 6 for 10 minutes until sizzling and starting to brown.

2. Put the flour and salt in a bowl. Add the egg and half the milk and water and whisk with a balloon whisk or beat with a wooden spoon until smooth. Stir in the remaining milk and water and add the herbs, if using.

3. Pour over the sausages and return to the oven for about 25 minutes until well risen, crisp and golden brown.

4. Serve hot with baked beans or canned tomatoes and, ideally, a leafy green vegetable.

Preparation time: 4–5 minutes
Cooking time: 35 minutes

SAUSAGE SALAD

Serves 2

Ingredients	Metric	Imperial	American
Slices of white bread, cubed	2	2	2
Oil	30 ml	2 tbsp	2 tbsp
Thick sausages, cooked and sliced	4	4	4
Can of sweetcorn (corn) with (bell) peppers, drained	300 g	11 oz	1 large
Can of butter beans, drained	425 g	15 oz	1 large
Cucumber, diced	¼	¼	¼
Garlic purée (paste)	1.5 ml	¼ tsp	¼ tsp
Plain yoghurt OR soured (dairy sour) cream	60 ml	4 tbsp	4 tbsp
Dried chives	5 ml	1 tsp	1 tsp
Salt and pepper			

I. **Fry (sauté) the cubes of bread in the hot oil until golden. Drain on kitchen paper.**

2. **Mix the sausages with the corn and peppers, butter beans and cucumber.**

3. **Mix the garlic purée with the yoghurt or soured cream, the chives and a little salt and pepper.**

4. **Add the fried bread to the salad and toss. Pile on to serving plates and add the creamy dressing on top.**

Preparation time: 10 minutes
Cooking time: 10 minutes
(for the sausages if necessary)

PEPPERAMI CARBONARA

Serves 2

Ingredients	Metric	Imperial	American
Spaghetti	175 g	6 oz	6 oz
Small onion, chopped	1	1	1
Oil	30 ml	2 tbsp	2 tbsp
Garlic purée (paste)	2.5 ml	½ tsp	½ tsp
Pepperami-style stick, chopped	1	1	1
Salt and pepper			
Chopped parsley	15 ml	1 tbsp	1 tbsp
OR dried chives	5 ml	1 tsp	1 tsp
Egg	1	1	1
Milk	15 ml	1 tbsp	1 tbsp

To serve: Parmesan or Cheddar cheese, grated

1. Cook the spaghetti according to the packet directions. Drain and return to the pan.

2. Meanwhile, fry (sauté) the onion in the oil for 1 minute. Add the garlic purée, pepperami, a little salt and pepper and the parsley or chives. Cover with a lid and cook gently for 5 minutes. Add to the pasta and toss well.

3. Beat the egg with the milk. Add to the pan and stir over a gentle heat until creamy and lightly scrambled.

4. Spoon on to serving plates and top with lots of grated cheese.

Preparation time: 10 minutes
Cooking time: 12 minutes

KNOCK-UP JAMBALAYA

Serves 2–4

Ingredients	Metric	Imperial	American
Long-grain rice	225 g	8 oz	1 cup
Dried onion flakes	15 ml	1 tbsp	1 tbsp
Dried green (bell) pepper flakes	15 ml	1 tbsp	1 tbsp
Chopped parsley (optional)	15 ml	1 tbsp	1 tbsp
Dried chives	2.5 ml	½ tsp	½ tsp
Garlic purée (paste)	1.5 ml	¼ tsp	¼ tsp
Salt and pepper			
Can of tomatoes	400 g	14 oz	1 large
Chicken or vegetable stock, made with 1 stock cube)	450 ml	3/4 pt	2 cups
Can of frankfurters, drained and cut into chunks	425 g	15 oz	1 large

1. **Mix all the ingredients except the frankfurters in a large frying pan (skillet).**

2. **Bring to the boil, reduce the heat, cover and simmer gently for 20 minutes.**

3. **Add the frankfurters and cook gently until hot through and the rice is tender and has absorbed all the liquid.**

4. **Serve straight from the pan.**

Preparation time: 5 minutes
Cooking time: 23 minutes

QUICK SMOKED SAUSAGE PILAF

Serves 2

Ingredients	Metric	Imperial	American
Long-grain rice	100 g	4 oz	½ cup
Frozen diced mixed vegetables	100 g	4 oz	1 cup
Knob of margarine			
Onion, finely chopped	1	1	1
Chilli powder (optional)	2.5 ml	½ tsp	½ tsp
Dried mixed herbs	2.5 ml	½ tsp	½ tsp
Smoked sausage, sliced	175 g	6 oz	6 oz
Salt and pepper			

1. Cook the rice in plenty of boiling lightly salted water for 10 minutes or until just tender. Add the vegetables after 5 minutes of cooking time. Drain, rinse with boiling water and drain again.

2. Meanwhile, melt the margarine in a large frying pan (skillet). Add the onion and fry (sauté), stirring, for about 4 minutes until lightly golden.

3. Stir in the chilli powder, if using, the herbs and the sausage. Heat through for 2 minutes, stirring.

4. Add the rice and vegetable mixture, season to taste and cook, stirring, until piping hot.

Preparation time: 5 minutes
Cooking time: 10–12 minutes

SAUERKRAUT WITH FRANKFURTERS

Serves 2

Ingredients	Metric	Imperial	American
Jar of sauerkraut	1	1	1
Caraway seeds	15 ml	1 tbsp	1 tbsp
Frankfurters	6–8	6–8	6–8

To serve: Potatoes and mustard

1. **Empty the sauerkraut into a saucepan. Add the caraway seeds and heat through. Drain.**

2. **Heat the frankfurters according to the packet directions.**

3. **Serve on hot plates with plain boiled potatoes and mustard. German or Dijon mustard go especially well.**

Preparation time: 4 minutes
Cooking time: 8 minutes

SPAGHETTI WITH BACON AND EGGS

You can use streaky bacon instead, but bacon pieces from the deli counter are much cheaper. Throw a few dried chives in for colour if you haven't any fresh parsley.

Serves 4

Ingredients	Metric	Imperial	American
Bacon pieces	50 g	2 oz	½ cup
Small onion, finely chopped	1	1	1
Garlic purée (paste)	2.5 ml	½ tsp	½ tsp
Oil	30 ml	2 tbsp	2 tbsp
Spaghetti	175 g	6 oz	6 oz
Chopped parsley (optional)	15 ml	1 tbsp	1 tbsp
Egg	1	1	1
Milk	30 ml	2 tbsp	2 tbsp
Salt and pepper			

To serve: Grated Cheddar or Parmesan cheese and salad

I. Cut the bacon pieces into small bits, discarding any rind or bone. Fry (sauté) the onion, garlic purée and bacon in the oil for 2 minutes, cover and cook gently for 5 minutes until the onion is soft.

2. Meanwhile, cook the spaghetti according to the packet directions, drain and return to the pan.

3. Stir in the bacon mixture and parsley, if using. Beat the egg with the milk and add to the pan. Toss over a gentle heat until creamy but do not boil or the egg will scramble. Season.

4. Serve with grated cheese and salad.

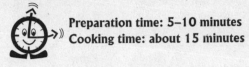

Preparation time: 5–10 minutes
Cooking time: about 15 minutes

PORK AND NOODLE STIR-FRY

Serves 2

Ingredients	Metric	Imperial	American
Quick-cook Chinese egg noodles	100 g	4 oz	4 oz
Belly pork slices	2	2	2
Oil	15 ml	1 tbsp	1 tbsp
Small onion, sliced	1	1	1
Carrot, cut into matchsticks	1	1	1
Small green (bell) pepper, cut into strips	1	1	1
Mushrooms, sliced	50 g	2 oz	2 oz
Cucumber, cut into matchsticks	¼	¼	¼
Vinegar	30 ml	2 tbsp	2 tbsp
Soy sauce	30 ml	2 tbsp	2 tbsp
Light brown sugar	15 ml	1 tbsp	1 tbsp
Ground ginger	5 ml	1 tsp	1 tsp
Salt and pepper			

1. **Cook the noodles according to the packet directions. Drain.**

2. **Using scissors, cut the rind and any bones off the pork and cut the meat into small pieces.**

3. **Heat the oil in a large pan or wok. Add the pork and fry (sauté) for 4 minutes, stirring.**

4. **Add the vegetables and continue cooking, stirring, for 5 minutes.**

5. Add the noodles and the remaining ingredients. Toss well until heated through. Taste and add a little more soy sauce or sugar, if liked. Serve straight away.

Preparation time: 10–15 minutes
Cooking time: 10 minutes

MACARONI MUNCH

Serves 2

Ingredients	Metric	Imperial	American
Bacon pieces	50 g	2 oz	½ cup
Quick-cook macaroni	100 g	4 oz	4 oz
Red Leicester or strong cheese, grated	100 g	4 oz	1 cup
Worcestershire sauce	5 ml	1 tsp	1 tsp
Salt and pepper			
Margarine	25 g	1 oz	2 tbsp

1. Remove any rind or bone from the bacon and cut into small pieces. Fry (sauté) with no extra fat until crisp.

2. Meanwhile, cook the macaroni according to the packet directions, drain and return to the pan.

3. Add the cheese, Worcestershire sauce, a little seasoning and the margarine. Toss well until creamy.

4. Pile on to warm serving plates and serve sprinkled with the bacon.

Preparation time: 5 minutes
Cooking time: about 10 minutes

ALMOST AUTHENTIC MOUSSAKA

Use minced (ground) beef instead of lamb if you prefer.

Serves 2

Ingredients	Metric	Imperial	American
Small onion, finely chopped	1	1	1
Garlic purée (paste)	2.5 ml	½ tsp	½ tsp
Minced (ground) lamb	175 g	6 oz	1½ cups
Water	150 ml	¼ pt	⅔ cup
Tomato purée (paste)	15 ml	1 tbsp	1 tbsp
Ground cinnamon or nutmeg	2.5 ml	½ tsp	½ tsp
Dried oregano or mixed herbs	2.5 ml	½ tsp	½ tsp
Salt and pepper			
Large potato, sliced	1	1	1
OR large courgette, sliced	1	1	1
Plain yoghurt	150 ml	¼ pt	⅔ cup
Egg	1	1	1
Cheddar cheese, grated	50 g	2 oz	½ cup

To serve: Pitta bread and salad

1. **Fry (sauté) the onion, garlic purée and mince together in a saucepan, stirring until the grains of meat are brown and separate.**

2. **Add the water and boil for about 5 minutes until nearly all the liquid has evaporated.**

3. Stir in the tomato purée, cinnamon or nutmeg and oregano or mixed herbs. Season to taste and simmer for 5 minutes.

4. Meanwhile, boil the potato or courgette in salted water for about 5 minutes or until tender. Drain.

5. Layer the meat mixture and the potato or courgette in a flameproof dish, finishing with a layer of potato.

6. Beat the yoghurt, egg and cheese together and spoon over the top. Place under a moderately hot grill (broiler) until the topping is set and golden, about 5 minutes.

7. Serve with pitta bread and salad.

Preparation time: 10 minutes
Cooking time: 20 minutes

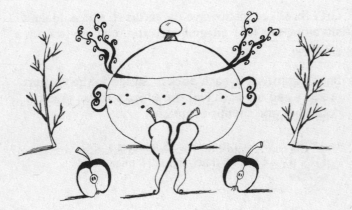

GREEK-STYLE LAMB LUNCH

Serves 2

Ingredients	Metric	Imperial	American
Frozen minced (ground) lambsteaks	2	2	2
Plain yoghurt	60 ml	4 tbsp	4 tbsp
Garlic purée (paste)	2.5 ml	½ tsp	½ tsp
Dried mint	2.5 ml	½ tsp	½ tsp
Salt and pepper			
Pitta bread	2	2	2

To serve: Shredded lettuce, grated cucumber and chopped tomato

1. Cook the lambsteaks according to the packet instructions.

2. Meanwhile, mix the yoghurt with the garlic purée, mint and a little salt and pepper.

3. Grill (broil) or microwave the pittas to warm. Make a slit along one long edge of each and open up to form a pocket.

4. Put a lambsteak in each pocket. Spoon in the yoghurt mixture and top each with shredded lettuce, grated cucumber and chopped tomato.

Preparation time: 5 minutes
Cooking time: about 10 minutes

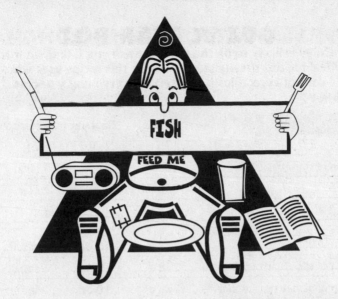

Brain food! Fish is incredibly good for you but can range from dirt cheap to staggeringly expensive. I've chosen the pick of the catch for high quality and low cost and have come up with some great ideas using canned fish, which is fantastically good value. The good thing about fish is that any type can be cooked in any way, so don't be afraid to experiment. You'll find mackerel and herring are very good buys but white fish varies enormously in cost. Coley, hake and huss are often relatively cheap, especially in frozen packs, but look out for special offers on the fresh fish counter.

QUICK FISH POT

Coley is likely to be the cheapest fish you'll find, so it is ideal for this speedy stew. Because this recipe uses whole cans of vegetables it will serve 2 very hungry people.

Serves 2

Ingredients	Metric	Imperial	American
Fresh or frozen white fish fillet	175 g	6 oz	6 oz
Can of tomatoes	400 g	14 oz	1 large
Water	150 ml	½ pt	⅔ cup
Vegetable stock cube	1	1	1
Can of new potatoes, drained and quartered	278 g	10 oz	1 small
Can of sliced carrots, drained	278 g	10 oz	1 small
Can of garden peas, drained	278 g	10 oz	1 small
Salt and pepper			

To serve: Crusty bread

1. Cut the fish into small chunks, discarding the skin and any bones.
2. Place the tomatoes in a large saucepan and break up with a wooden spoon. Add the remaining ingredients, adding the fish last.
3. Bring to the boil, reduce the heat, cover and simmer for 5 minutes until the fish is tender. Stir gently and season to taste. Ladle into large, warm soup bowls and serve with lots of crusty bread.

Preparation time: 3 minutes
Cooking time: 5 minutes

Variation: Even Quicker Fish Pot
Prepare as above but substitute 120 g/4½ oz/1 small can of pilchards in tomato sauce (roughly cut up the fish) for the white fish and just bring to the boil.

THAI FISH FILLETS

Thin fillets such as whiting or flat fish such as plaice or dab are good for this dish. Look out for the bargain of the week on the fish counter.

Serves 2

Ingredients	Metric	Imperial	American
White fish fillets, skinned, about 150 g/5 oz each	2	2	2
Salt	2–5 ml	½–1 tsp	½–1 tsp
Coarsely grated rind and juice of 1 lime			
Light brown suger	30 ml	2 tbsp	2 tbsp
To serve:			
Rice cooked with peas and seasoned with a pinch of chilli powder			

1. Sprinkle the fillets with the salt and lime juice and leave to marinate for **20–25 minutes**.

2. Sprinkle with sugar and grill (broil) for about **5 minutes** until the fillets are cooked and the sugar has caramelised.

3. Serve on a bed of rice and peas, garnished with the lime rind.

Preparation time: 2–3 minutes, plus marinating
Cooking time: 5 minutes

MUSTARD MACKEREL

Serves 2

Ingredients	Metric	Imperial	American
Whole mackerel, cleaned	2	2	2
Salt and pepper			
Margarine	40 g	1½ oz	3 tbsp
Oil	10 ml	2 tsp	2 tsp
Mustard	5 ml	1 tsp	1 tsp
Caster (superfine) sugar	1.5 ml	¼ tsp	¼ tsp
Vinegar or lemon juice	2.5 ml	½ tsp	½ tsp
Salt and pepper			

To serve: Potatoes and broad (lima) beans

1. Cut the heads off the mackerel if you prefer, and wipe inside and out with kitchen paper. Slash the fish in several places along each side with a sharp knife and season with salt and pepper.

2. Heat 15 g/½ oz/1 tbsp of the margarine with the oil in a large frying pan (skillet).

3. Add the fish and fry (sauté) for about 5 minutes on each side until browned and cooked through. (You can serve just like this if you wish.)

4. Remove the fish from the pan, drain on kitchen paper and transfer to warm serving plates.

5. Add the remaining margarine to the pan juices with the mustard, sugar, vinegar or lemon juice, and a little salt and pepper. Stir until melted and bubbling.

6. Pour over the fish. Serve with potatoes and broad beans.

Preparation time: 10 minutes
Cooking time: 10 minutes

MACKEREL MANIA

Serves 2

Ingredients	Metric	Imperial	American
Pasta shapes	100 g	4 oz	4 oz
Frozen peas	50 g	2 oz	½ cup
Can of mackerel steaks, drained	185 g	6½ oz	1 small
Can of cream of tomato soup	295 g	10½ oz	1 small
Dried basil	2.5 ml	½ tsp	½ tsp

1. Cook the pasta according to the packet directions. Add the frozen peas after 5 minutes, then continue cooking until the pasta is cooked. Drain and return to the saucepan.

2. Discard any skin and bones from the mackerel. Break up and add to the pasta with the soup and the basil. Heat through, stirring gently until piping hot.

3. Pile on to plates and serve immediately.

Preparation time: 3 minutes
Cooking time: 12 minutes

FISH PROVENCALE

Cod is the classic but any white fish will do.

Serves 2

Ingredients	Metric	Imperial	American
Garlic purée (paste)	2.5 ml	½ tsp	½ tsp
Can of tomatoes	400 g	14 oz	1 large
Tomato purée (paste)	15 ml	1 tbsp	1 tbsp
White fish fillet, skinned and cubed	225 g	8 oz	8 oz
Salt and pepper			

To serve: Plain boiled rice and mixed salad or green beans

1. Put the garlic purée and tomatoes in a pan and break up with a wooden spoon.

2. Add the tomato purée, bring to the boil and boil rapidly for 5 minutes, stirring occasionally.

3. Add the fish and cook gently for 3–5 minutes until the fish is cooked but not breaking up.

4. Season to taste and serve on a bed of boiled rice, with a mixed salad or green beans.

Preparation time: 10 minutes
Cooking time: 10–15 minutes

FISH AND POTATO FRY

Serves 2

Ingredients	Metric	Imperial	American
Oil	15 ml	1 tbsp	1 tbsp
Large potatoes, grated	2	2	2
Any white fish fillet, skinned and cubed	225 g	8 oz	8 oz
Salt and pepper			
Can of tomatoes	400 g	14 oz	1 large

To serve: Peas

1. Heat the oil in a frying pan (skillet).

2. Add half the potatoes and press down well. Season.

3. Add the fish in a layer, then top with the remaining potatoes, press down and season.

4. Cover with a lid or foil and cook gently for **20 minutes** or until cooked through.

5. Meanwhile, heat the tomatoes in a pan with a little pepper.

6. Turn the fish and potato fry out on to a warmed serving plate.

7. Serve cut in half with the tomatoes and peas.

Preparation time: 10 minutes
Cooking time: 20 minutes

CAESAR SALAD SPECIAL

Serves 2–3

Ingredients	Metric	Imperial	American
Knob of margarine			
Egg, beaten	1	1	1
Soft garlic and herb cheese	75 g	3 oz	⅓ cup
Milk	45 ml	3 tbsp	3 tbsp
Oil	15 ml	1 tbsp	1 tbsp
Vinegar or lemon juice	10 ml	2 tsp	2 tsp
Small iceberg lettuce	½	½	½
Can of tuna, drained and chopped	85 g	3½ oz	1 small
Slices of French bread, fried (sautéed) in a little oil	4	4	4

To garnish: Tomato wedges

1. **Melt the margarine in a pan. Add the egg and scramble lightly over a gentle heat. Remove the heat and leave to cool.**

2. **Whisk the cheese with the milk, oil and vinegar or lemon juice until smooth.**

3. **Tear the lettuce into neat pieces. Place in a salad bowl.**

4. **Add the egg and tuna, pour over the cheese mixture and toss.**

5. **Arrange slices of fried French bread around the edges of the bowl and garnish with tomato wedges.**

Preparation time: 15 minutes
Cooking time: nil

ONE-POT KEDGEREE

'Golden cutlets' are usually the cheapest yellow smoked fish, but smoked mackerel is often reasonably priced, too.

Serves 2

Ingredients	Metric	Imperial	American
Eggs, scrubbed under cold water	2	2	2
Long-grain rice	100 g	4 oz	½ cup
Salt			
Turmeric (optional)	5 ml	1 tsp	1 tsp
Smoked fish fillet	100 g	4 oz	4 oz
Frozen peas	50 g	2 oz	½ cup
Milk	20 ml	4 tsp	4 tsp
Pepper			
Grated nutmeg (optional)			

1. Put the eggs in a large pan of water and bring to the boil. Add the rice, a little salt and the turmeric, if using. Bring back to the boil and boil for 5 minutes.

2. Add the fish and peas and cook for a further 5 minutes.

3. Remove the fish and eggs. Drain the rice and peas and return to the saucepan.

4. Break up the fish, discard the skin and any bones. Shell the eggs and roughly cut up.

5. Add the fish and eggs to the rice and peas with the milk, salt and pepper and the nutmeg, if using. Heat through.

Preparation time: 10 minutes
Cooking time: 12 minutes

ALMOST PAELLA

Cook enough for 4 people rather than splitting a
packet of savoury rice. Eat any leftovers cold the next day
but do not reheat.

Serves 3–4

Ingredients	Metric	Imperial	American
Packet of savoury mushroom or vegetable rice	1	1	1
Boiling water	450 ml	¾ pt	2 cups
Cooked chicken, diced	100 g	4 oz	1 cup
Can of mussels, drained	250 g	9 oz	1 small
To serve: Crusty bread			
Salad			

1. Put the rice in a pan with the boiling water. Stir, cover and simmer for 12 minutes.

2. Add the remaining ingredients, stir, cover and simmer gently for a further 8 minutes until all the liquid has been absorbed and the rice is tender.

3. Serve with crusty bread and salad.

Preparation time: 4 minutes
Cooking time: 20 minutes

TIP: Make this go round for another 1 or 2 people by adding a drained can of sweetcorn (corn), haricot (navy) beans, or tuna towards the end of cooking.

TUNA AND CORN PASTA

Serves 4

Ingredients	Metric	Imperial	American
Pasta shapes	225 g	8 oz	8 oz
Packet of cheese sauce mix and milk according to the directions	1	1	1
OR 1 quantity of cheese sauce (see Basic Macaroni Cheese, page 49)			
Can of tuna, drained	185 g	6½ oz	1 small
Can of sweetcorn (corn), drained	200 g	7 oz	1 small
To serve: Cheddar cheese, grated (optional) and a green salad			

I. Cook the pasta according to the packet directions, then drain.

2. Meanwhile, make the cheese sauce. Add the drained tuna and sweetcorn, stir and heat through.

3. Add the drained pasta and toss well. Spoon on to plates.

4. Serve topped with a little grated cheese, if liked, and salad.

 Preparation time: 2 minutes
Cooking time: 10–12 minutes

TIP: If reheating the next day, add a little milk to the saucepan and stir all the time over a moderate heat.

FISH CREOLE

Serves 2

Ingredients	Metric	Imperial	American
White fish fillets, skinned (about 150 g/5 oz each)	2	2	2
Plain (all-purpose) flour	15 ml	1 tbsp	1 tbsp
Salt and pepper			
Chilli powder	2.5 ml	½ tsp	½ tsp
Margarine	15 g	½ oz	1 tbsp
Oil	15 ml	1 tbsp	1 tbsp
Banana, cut into chunks	1	1	1
To garnish (optional): Lime or lemon wedges			
To serve: Plain boiled rice and a green salad			

1. **Dust the fish with flour mixed with a little salt and pepper and the chilli powder. (Use a little less chilli powder if you don't like food too spicy.)**

2. **Heat half the margarine and the oil in a frying pan (skillet) and fry (sauté) the fish for 3 minutes on each side until lightly golden and cooked through.**

3. **Transfer to a warm serving dish and keep warm.**

4. **Add the remaining margarine and oil to the pan and stir-fry the banana until softening (about 2 minutes). Transfer to the serving dish.**

5. **Garnish with lime or lemon wedges, if liked, and serve hot with rice and a green salad.**

Preparation time: 5 minutes
Cooking time: 8 minutes

EXTRA ENERGY FODDER

FEED ME

Get yourself geared up to make a batch of any of the following before you have to get stuck into revising or serious exam schedules. Then you'll have something highly comforting and packed with a great energy boost for when your spirits are flagging or you simply haven't got time to stop for a proper meal (like breakfast when you've overslept from all that study...or whatever!). None of them takes long to make and they are all far cheaper than buying equivalent bars in the supermarket or health food shop.

PEANUT HONEY BITES

These biscuits make a nutritious snack when serious study is at hand.

Makes 12

Ingredients	Metric	Imperial	American
Hard block margarine	75 g	3 oz	⅓ cup
Thick honey	45 ml	3 tbsp	3 tbsp
Plain biscuits (cookies), crushed	225 g	8 oz	2 cups
Grated lemon rind (optional)	5 ml	1 tsp	1 tsp
Crunchy peanut butter	45 ml	3 tbsp	3 tbsp

1. **Melt the margarine with the honey and bring to the boil. Remove from the heat.**

2. **Stir in the remaining ingredients and mix well.**

3. **Press into a greased 18 cm/7 in square baking tin and chill until set. Cut into squares and store in airtight tin.**

Preparation time: 10 minutes, plus chilling
Cooking time: nil

CHEWY APRICOT BARS

**These bars are great energy boosters
during cramming sessions.**

Makes 15

Ingredients	Metric	Imperial	American
Can of evaporated milk	175 g	6 oz	1 small
Thick honey	20 ml	4 tsp	4 tsp
Apple juice	45 ml	3 tbsp	3 tbsp
Hard block margarine	50 g	2 oz	¼ cup
Light brown sugar	50 g	2 oz	¼ cup
Sultanas (golden raisins)	100 g	4 oz	⅔ cup
Ready-to-eat dried apricots, chopped	225 g	8 oz	1½ cups
Desiccated (shredded) coconut	100 g	4 oz	1 cup
Rolled oats	225 g	8 oz	2 cups

1. **Heat the evaporated milk with the honey, apple juice, margarine and sugar until just melted. Remove from the heat.**

2. **Add the remaining ingredients and mix well. Press into a greased 28 × 18 cm/11 × 7 in baking tin.**

3. **Wrap in clingfilm (plastic wrap) or put in a clean plastic carrier bag and chill overnight to allow the flavours to develop before cutting into bars.**

4. **Store in an airtight container in the fridge.**

**Preparation time: 5 minutes, plus chilling
Cooking time: nil**

CINNAMON FRENCH TOAST

Comfort food at its best! To turn into a really nutritious snack, cut an apple into wedges or a banana into chunks to eat with the toast.

Serves 2

Ingredients	Metric	Imperial	American
Egg	1	1	1
Milk	30 ml	2 tbsp	2 tbsp
Thick slices of bread, crusts removed	4	4	4
Margarine	25 g	1 oz	2 tbsp
Oil	30 ml	2 tbsp	2 tbsp
Caster (superfine) sugar	20 ml	4 tsp	4 tsp
Cinnamon	5 ml	1 tsp	1 tsp

1. Beat the egg and milk together. Dip the bread in to coat it completely.

2. Heat the margarine and oil in a large frying pan (skillet). Fry (sauté) the slices for about 1½ minutes over a high heat until a deep golden brown, turning once.

3. Drain on kitchen paper.

4. Mix the sugar and cinnamon on a flat plate. Dip the bread into the mixture until coated on both sides. Serve straight away cut into triangles.

Preparation time: 2 minutes
Cooking time: 3 minutes

NO-BAKE CRUNCH BARS

OK, so chocolate isn't very good for you, but as a source of energy and a terrific taste these are a must during revision periods.

Makes 12–16

Ingredients	Metric	Imperial	American
Hard block margarine	175 g	6 oz	¾ cup
Light brown sugar	50 g	2 oz	¼ cup
Golden (light corn) syrup	30 ml	2 tbsp	2 tbsp
Cocoa (unsweetened chocolate) powder	45 ml	3 tbsp	3 tbsp
Raisins	75 g	3 oz	½ cup
Oat crunch-type cereal	350 g	12 oz	3 cups
Plain (semi-sweet) cooking chocolate	200 g	7 oz	7 oz

1. Oil and line the base of an 18 × 28 cm/7 × 11 in baking tin (pan) with baking parchment, greaseproof (waxed) paper or the inside wrapper from a cereal packet.

2. Melt the margarine, sugar and syrup and cocoa in a pan. Remove from the heat. Stir in the raisins and cereal. Press into the tin.

3. Melt the chocolate in a pan over hot water and spread over the top, right into the corners.

4. Chill until set, cut into fingers and store in a airtight tin.

Preparation time: 5 minutes, plus chilling
Cooking time: nil

THE EASIEST FLAPJACKS

These are great to grab on the way out in the morning when there's no time for breakfast!

Makes 12

Ingredients	Metric	Imperial	American
Soft margarine	75 g	3 oz	⅓ cup
Light brown sugar	75 g	3 oz	⅓ cup
Rolled oats	100 g	4 oz	1 cup
Mixed (apple pie) spice (optional)	5 ml	1 tsp	1 tsp

1. Beat all the ingredients together until well mixed.

2. Turn into a greased 18 cm/7 in tin and press down well. Bake in a preheated oven at 220°C/425°F/gas mark 7 for 15–20 minutes until golden.

3. Leave to cool in the tin for 10 minutes, then cut into pieces. Leave in the tin until completely cold before removing. Store in an airtight tin.

Preparation time: 3 minutes
Cooking time: 15–20 minutes

DODDLE DESSERTS

FEED ME

If you're health-conscious, you'll live off yoghurts or fresh fruit for afters which is a great idea and it's economical. But every now and then you might hanker after a real pud – a bit of comfort food once again. Here are some dead easy ideas which taste terrific and are ideal for filling up on – especially when you have some friends around for a meal.

RHUBARB AND CUSTARD CHARLOTTE

Serves 4–5

Ingredients	Metric	Imperial	American
Margarine, melted	25 g	1 oz	2 tbsp
Slices of bread and margarine	4	4	4
Individual carton of custard	1	1	1
Can of rhubarb, drained, reserving the juice	550 g	1 lb 4 oz	1 large
Light brown sugar	30 ml	1 tbsp	1 tbsp

1. **Grease an ovenproof dish with half the melted margarine.**

2. **Line the dish with 2½ slices of the bread.**

3. **Spread the custard in the base, then top with the drained fruit.**

4. **Dice the remaining bread, toss in melted margarine and sugar and spoon over.**

5. **Bake in a preheated oven at 200°C/400°F/gas mark 6 for about 40 minutes until golden. Serve with the reserved juice.**

Preparation time: 5 minutes
Cooking time: 40 minutes

BLACK FOREST RICE

Serves 4

Ingredients	Metric	Imperial	American
Can of cherry pie filling	410 g	14½ oz	1 large
Can of chocolate rice pudding	425 g	15 oz	1 large
Can of cream	200 g	7 oz	1 small
To decorate:			
Grated chocolate or drinking (sweetened) chocolate powder			

1. Layer the cherry pie filling and chocolate rice in 4 glasses.

2. Drain any whey off the cream and pipe or spoon a swirl of cream in each dish.

3. Sprinkle the grated chocolate or drinking chocolate powder. Chill before serving, if you have time.

 Preparation time: 3 minutes
Cooking time: nil

Variation: Summer Rice
Prepare as for Black Forest Rice but substitute a can of strawberry pie filling for the cherry and plain creamed rice pudding for the chocolate rice. Decorate with chopped nuts, if liked.

PINEAPPLE UPSIDE-DOWN PUDDING

This pudding is just as good cold as hot.

Serves 6

Ingredients	Metric	Imperial	American
Knob of margarine			
Light brown sugar	30 ml	2 tbsp	2 tbsp
Can of pineapple rings, drained, reserving the juice	225 g	8 oz	1 small
Glacé (candied) cherries, halved OR a few sultanas (golden raisins)			
Packet sponge cake mix	1	1	1
Egg and water according to the packet directions			

I. Liberally grease a 20 cm/8 in round sandwich tin (pan) or other shallow ovenproof dish with the margarine.

2. Sprinkle the sugar over the base, then top with the pineapple rings.

3. Place a halved glacé cherry, cut side up, in the centre of each ring, or a few sultanas or raisins here and in the gaps around.

4. Make up the sponge mixture according to the packet directions. Spoon over the fruit.

5. Bake in a preheated oven at 190°C/375°F/gas mark 5 for 20 minutes until risen so that the centre springs back when lightly pressed.

6. Leave to cool slightly in the tin, then loosen the edges with a round-bladed knife and turn out on to a serving plate. Serve with the juice.

Preparation time: 8 minutes
Cooking time: 20 minutes

MOCK RUM BABAS

Serves 6

Ingredients	Metric	Imperial	American
Sugar	100 g	4 oz	½ cup
Water	150 ml	¼ pt	⅔ cup
Rum OR rum essence (extract) and water	30 ml	2 tbsp	2 tbsp
Ring doughnuts	6	6	6
Aerosol cream, cream substitute or fromage frais			
Chopped nuts (optional)			

1. Dissolve the sugar in the water. Boil for 5 minutes until syrupy.

2. Stir in the rum or rum essence and water.

3. Prick the doughnuts all over with a skewer and spoon rum syrup over them. Leave to soak well. Chill if you have time.

4. Just before serving, fill the centres with cream or fromage frais and decorate with nuts, if liked.

Preparation time: 2 minutes
Cooking time: 5 minutes, plus chilling

CARAMEL APPLES

Serves 4

Ingredients	Metric	Imperial	American
Margarine	50 g	2 oz	¼ cup
Eating (dessert) apples, sliced	4	4	4
Light brown sugar	50 g	2 oz	¼ cup
Mixed (apple pie) spice	2.5 ml	1 tsp	1 tsp
Sultanas (golden raisins)	25 g	1 oz	2 tbsp

To serve: Whipped cream or yoghurt

1. **Melt the margarine in a frying pan (skillet).**

2. **Add the apples and sprinkle with the sugar. Fry (sauté), tossing occasionally, for about 3 minutes until the sugar has melted.**

3. **Add the mixed spice and the sultanas and toss gently. Serve with whipped cream or yoghurt.**

Preparation time: 5 minutes
Cooking time: 5 minutes

BANANAS WITH HOT LEMON SAUCE

Serves 2

Ingredients	Metric	Imperial	American
Margarine	25 g	1 oz	2 tbsp
Light brown sugar	40 g	1½ oz	3 tbsp
Lemon juice	15 ml	1 tbsp	1 tbsp
Plain yoghurt OR ice cream	150 ml	¼ pt	⅔ cup
Bananas			

1. Put the margarine, sugar and lemon juice in a small pan. Heat gently, stirring until the sugar has melted. Simmer for one minute.

2. Divide the yoghurt or ice cream between 2 glasses. Top with sliced bananas.

3. Spoon the sauce over and serve straight away.

 Preparation time: 5 minutes
Cooking time: about 3 minutes

NO-EFFORT CRUMBLE

Serves 3–4

Ingredients	Metric	Imperial	American
Can of fruit, drained, reserving the juice	410 g	14½ oz	1 large
Margarine	50 g	2 oz	¼ cup
Weetabix	2	2	2
Light brown sugar	15 ml	1 tbsp	1 tbsp
Ground ginger, cinnamon or mixed (apple pie) spice	2.5 ml	½ tsp	½ tsp

To serve: Cream or custard

1. **Put the fruit in an ovenproof dish.**

2. **Melt the margarine in a saucepan. Crumble the Weetabix and mix with the sugar and spice.**

3. **Sprinkle over the fruit, pressing down lightly. Bake in a preheated oven at 190°C/375°F/gas mark 5 for about 15 minutes until crisp. Serve warm with cream or custard.**

Preparation time: 3 minutes
Cooking time: 15 minutes

TOFFEE PLUM CHARLOTTE

When home-grown plums are plentiful this is a really cheap dessert. Alternatively, use peeled, cored and sliced cooking apples or pears.

Serves 4

Ingredients	Metric	Imperial	American
Margarine	50 g	2 oz	¼ cup
Light brown sugar	225 g	8 oz	1 cup
Lemon juice	15 ml	1 tbsp	1 tbsp
Slices of bread, cut thickly from a large loaf, crusts removed and cubed	4	4	4
Ripe plums, quartered and stones removed	450 g	1 lb	1 lb

To serve: Cream, yoghurt or fromage frais

1. **Melt the margarine in a large heavy-based frying pan (skillet). Add the sugar and stir over a gentle heat until the sugar has dissolved. Add the lemon juice.**

2. **Gently fold the bread through the toffee mixture until completely coated. Add the plums, cover and cook for about 5 minutes until the fruit is soft.**

3. **Serve hot or chilled with cream, yoghurt for fromage frais.**

Preparation time: 10–15 minutes
Cooking time: 8–10 minutes

INDEX

FEED ME